The First Time Dad's Newborn Guide

How to be the Best Father and Partner During Baby's First Year

Table of Contents

Table of Contents

Introduction

You might have come across memes as well as online posts about why children shouldn't be left alone with their dads. Dads are funny and they are believed to be the "cool" parents. Innocently drawing eyebrows on your little one to make them seem more expressive to using zip ties as scrunchies, dads can be quite funny. They certainly have a wide variety of hilarious tricks they get up to when left alone with their babies. Well, these instances might make you chuckle, but it sends a rather unfortunate message. An underlying message here is that fathers do not take their parenting responsibilities as seriously as mothers do.

Oh boy, this doesn't sound right. After all, we aren't living in the 1950s anymore. Long gone are the days when dads were busy smoking cigars while their wives were delivering babies. These days, fathers want to be more present. They want to play a significant part in parenting as well as their children's lives. The general perception of society toward parents is changing too. One such change is associated with how we view dads today. Dads are expected to be more hands-on. Well, expectations don't translate to knowledge or understanding. So, it isn't surprising that even though it isn't the 1950s, dads can still be clueless about babies. I believe it is time to break this stereotype of dads being incompetent. Isn't it time to put all running jokes about dads being less knowledgeable than moms to rest?

Becoming a parent is not only a significant milestone but is a life-changing experience too. From now on, your life will no longer be the same. You are not just responsible for yourself, but your child as well. The thing with parenting is, it is one role you never stop playing. Regardless of how old your child is, you will not stop being their parent. Once a parent, always a parent— and do not forget this. That said, becoming acquainted with this role is not easy.

Until you hold your baby in your arms for the first time, it will not sink in that you are now a father. This is a moment you will never forget. Now, you not only have a baby, but your baby has a father too. Regardless of how much you have read about pregnancy and prepared for it, moving onto this stage can leave you feeling unprepared. After all, until now, you were only reading about how to handle the pregnancy and what to expect. You are now holding a living and breathing little human being and all that reading might not have prepared you for this moment. Until now.

Becoming a parent is an overwhelming experience, even more so when this is your first experience. Chances are, you have a host of questions, doubts, and concerns about your role as a father. You are probably worried your partner has to do all the heavy lifting and you don't know what to do. Maybe you're worried about making mistakes or doing something that will harm your baby. Perhaps you don't know how to hold or soothe your baby. You want to be a good father and a partner, but don't know how to handle the newborn or what to do in this new role you have assumed only now. You might be worried about bonding with your baby or desire to reduce your spouse's load. You might be fixating on ensuring your family is off to a good start. Perhaps the biggest doubt playing on a loop in your head right now is whether you are being a good father or not.

Well, all this can be incredibly overwhelming. Taking care of your baby, learning to keep them safe, bringing them home for the first time, ensuring they are well fed and rested, soothing them, and dealing with emergencies are all a part of your job description now.

I fully understand how you are feeling. The good news is, with a little information and guidance, you can reduce any anxiety associated with becoming a first-time dad. The worries, fears, or doubts you have can also be effectively silenced. If even lessening the anxiety is your only goal this is the perfect book for you. In this book, all your questions and doubts about handling your newborn will be answered in detail. These pages are filled with plenty of tips and advice that can be used to improve your confidence as a new father. Apart from this, you will learn how to become an effective support system your partner needs in parenting. It's not only about taking care of your newborn, becoming the support system for your partner is equally important in fatherhood. Helping her get accustomed to this change while you are transitioning into parenthood is also needed. There is plenty to do and a lot to learn.

This book will act as your comprehensive guide while getting adjusted to your new role as a father. Firstly, you will learn about what to expect after your child is born, bringing the baby home from the hospital, and all the different processes involved in this journey. Your baby's developmental milestones, suggestions you can use to help your partner recover from childbirth, and advice to ensure that you become your partner's support system are also covered. You will also learn about the basics of taking care of your newborn from breastfeeding to bottle feeding and things to avoid. We have pretty much everything associated with taking care of your baby.

You will also learn about how to hold, feed, bathe and soothe your baby. Babies grow quite quickly; after reading you will know what to expect and how to help your baby develop and grow. When you are armed with all the information, suggestions, and advice given in this book, you can become the best father you can be. You can become the father your baby needs. You can also become a more understanding and caring partner. Knowledge makes all the difference in life, especially when it comes to overcoming fears. Are you wondering how I know all this? Well, I know this from personal experience. Hello! I'm a proud father of three wonderful kids. Parenthood is certainly a milestone and it changes your life in ways you cannot fully anticipate. That said, it is incredibly rewarding and satisfying. When you do anything for the first time can be scary and overwhelming, especially when there's a massive shift in responsibilities.

I remember I was quite young when our first child was born. I remember feeling simultaneously overwhelmed and helpless. I was fortunate enough that my parents were there to help prepare me and my wife through the entire process. Learning about what to expect during and after pregnancy helped reduce my helplessness while making me feel more in control of the situation. Knowing what to do reduces the uncertainties associated with becoming a first-time dad. Even though your partner is physically experiencing the pregnancy, it's a journey you are a part of as well. It is a truly magical experience. Raising three children has taught me a lot about parenthood as well as everything associated with pregnancy.

If you are worried as a first-time dad, you can rest easy because you are not alone. If you were scared, anxious, or have a bunch of questions about what to expect, this book is here for you. All the advice given in this book stems from my personal experience. Being a father of three kids has given me guidance on what to expect. This topic is quite close to my heart. My personal experience coupled with all the years I spent researching pregnancy and what to expect as a first-time parent has taught me so much. When I started sharing my personal experiences with others, I realized I had something to offer. I know how difficult it can be, especially when this is your first time. I know that everyone is capable of becoming a good father, regardless of their experience. All you need is a little guidance. Well, I have got your back; here to guide you every step of the way.

So, do you want to learn what you can expect as a first-time parent? Do you want to be the best father and partner you can be? Or maybe we're just curious to learn about what you can expect as a first-time parent. Well, the information given in this book will make the process seem less overwhelming and equip you with all the information needed. Once you know what to expect, preparing yourself becomes easier. When all this is in place, the transition into parenthood will seem less overwhelming. You can overcome any challenge that life throws your way, provided you know what to do.

So, what are you waiting for? Let us get started immediately!

Chapter 1: From Hospital to Home

This is the moment you and your partner were eagerly waiting for! Whether you are with your partner in the room while she's delivering the baby or anxiously pacing outside the operating theater, it's time for the big reveal — your baby is here! Congratulations, your baby is finally here! Now what? This is one question that is a source of anxiety and stress for first-time parents. Well, with a little preparation and the right information, this transition will become easy!

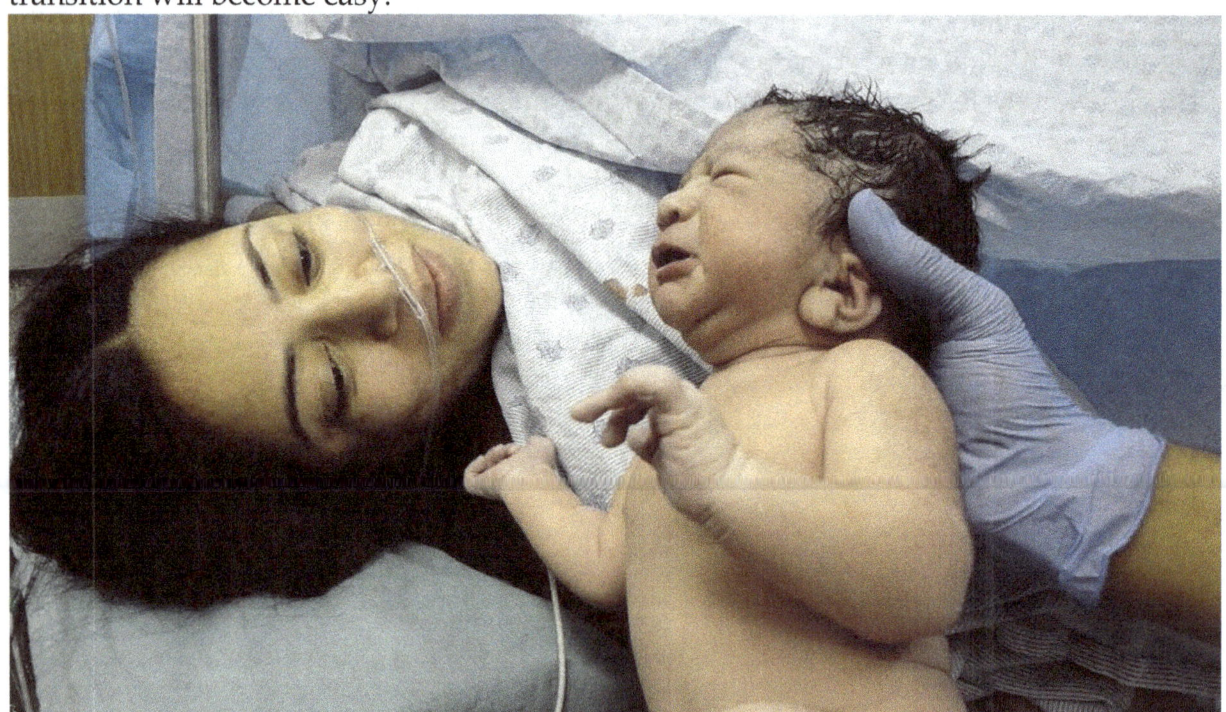

What Happens Right After Birth

If it is a vaginal birth without any complications, the mother will deliver the placenta soon after delivering the baby. A Pitocin injection will be administered to speed up this process. If there are any vaginal tears or a surgical cut made between the vagina and the anus known as episiotomy, the doctor will stitch it using a local anesthetic. In the meanwhile, a team of healthcare professionals will be tending to your newborn.
The first thing they will do is gently suction the nose and throat to unclog it and remove any mucus or amniotic fluids present in the airways. After this, a vitamin K injection will be administered to promote blood clotting. To prevent infections, an antibiotic ointment will be applied to the baby's eyes.

Basic exams to check your baby's reflexes and vital signs will be performed. The baby will also receive an Apgar score that assesses their heart rate, muscle tone, reflex response, breathing, and color. This essentially describes your baby's condition right after birth. It is normal and this is nothing to worry about. Your baby will be footprinted and an identification band will be placed on their leg and wrist.

Some parents might opt for skin-to-skin contact right after the baby's birth. This is a great time for the new mum to get accustomed to breastfeeding and holding her baby. This also promotes the uterus to contract and restricts bleeding after delivery.

C-Section

When the baby is delivered through a surgical operation it is known as a cesarean section or C-section. If your partner undergoes a C-section, the surgeon will take some time stitching her up after delivering the baby and the placenta. She will then be transferred to a recovery room for further monitoring for an hour or so. After this, she will be shifted to the maternity ward or the postpartum room. While she is going through all this, you will get additional time to take care of your little one.

Homebirth

If your partner opts for a home birth, the midwife will stay with her until she is confident the mother and baby are both stable. She will also help your partner start breastfeeding or bottle-feeding the baby. Apart from this, don't forget to check with her about support over the next couple of weeks.

Transfer to the Postpartum Room

Most hospitals these days encourage parents to room with their babies. It essentially means the baby will be sleeping in a bassinet or co-sleeper next to the mother's bed. This arrangement gives the mother a chance to bond with her newborn. Apart from this, it also encourages breastfeeding sessions to start according to the baby's needs. As parents, the first couple of hours after birth are precious. It gives you an incredible opportunity to bond with your baby.

That said, it is perfectly okay if your partner wants to sleep for a couple of hours and rest while the baby is in the nursery. You can take care of your infant while giving your partner a chance to rest. This is crucial right now. Why don't you also make the most of this opportunity and catch up on some sleep while the baby rests in the nursery?

Complications

Don't get scared hearing the term complications. At times, there are some complications during labor and birth. It means, the mother and the baby need some form of additional intervention or attention. In such situations, the baby might be transferred to a special unit for a higher level of care such as the Special Care Nursery (SCN) or the Neonatal Intensive Care Unit (NICU) at the hospital. If the baby was born before the 34 weeks of the gestation period, they are said to be premature. In such instances, the baby will need to stay at the hospital for a while longer.
It can be physically and emotionally challenging to deal with additional complications after delivery. Remember, it is extremely stressful for your partner right now and you need to be calm. Ensure you have an excellent healthcare team on standby and you keep your partner updated about the progress. If your baby is transferred to a separate unit, ensure you regularly visit the baby and update the new mom about the same.

What to Do With Your Newborn Baby

Skin-to-skin contact is not only comforting for the baby but is a special bonding experience for the parents as well. It's not just your partner. You should hold, care for, and softly talk to your newborn. This is quite a comforting experience for the newborn. If it is an uncomplicated vaginal delivery, the baby will be directly placed on the mother's belly after delivery.
Newborns are incredibly alert after birth and their first instinct is to seek out the mother's breast. If you and your partner have decided to go with the breastfeeding route, ensure she breastfeeds the baby within the first hour. This is because the initial breast milk produced is known as colostrum and is filled with antibodies your baby needs. Even if skin-to-skin contact or breastfeeding is not possible immediately, these can be taken care of later.
If your partner has delivered through a cesarean section, she can hold the baby right at the operating table itself. This also allows her to breastfeed the baby immediately after the operation. Dear first-time dad, the time your partner spends away from the little one allows you to bond. So, make the most of it.

Chances are, you'll have eager and excited family members as well as friends who are waiting outside the delivery room. Or maybe they are expecting a phone call. For now, your only priority is to concentrate on your partner and baby. Everything else can wait. Make the most of this time to bond. You can pass on the information even a while later. Spending quality time together as a new family is important.

While You're Still in the Hospital

Your bundle of joy is here! While you are still in the hospital, there are a couple of things you must do while your partner rests. She just went through an experience that is both exciting and tiring. So, it is time for you to step up as a new father! Here are some things you must do while at the hospital.

The most important thing is to ensure your partner sees a lactation consultant. Even if everything is going well with the baby, the consultant's insights about breastfeeding and postnatal care for your baby will be helpful. Some consultants might also agree to make home visits. Select an option that is comfortable for your partner.

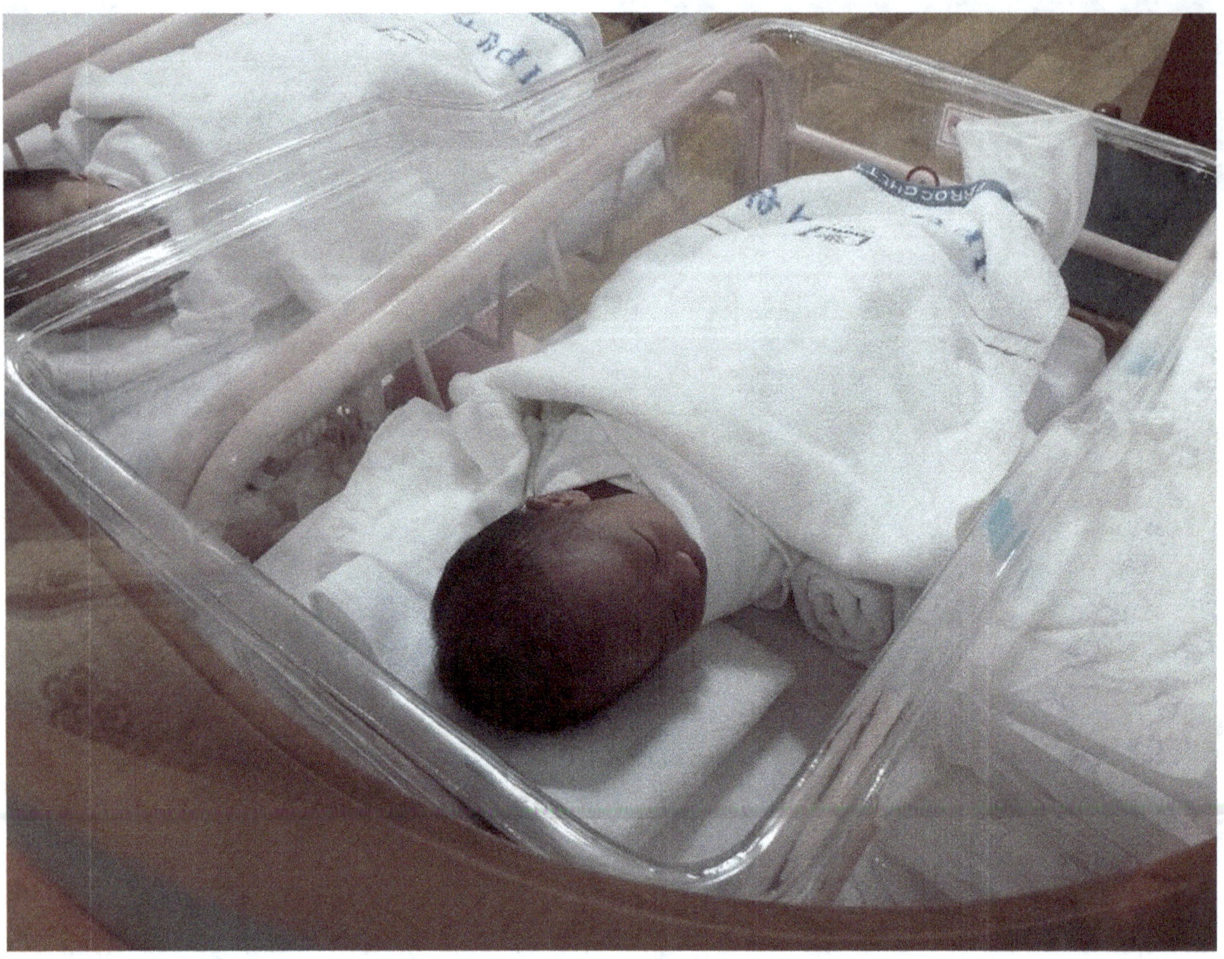

If your partner wants to bathe or even use the restroom after delivery, ensure that you accompany her. Post-delivery fainting is common. Delivering a baby is a physically excruciating experience for the mother and her body will need time to recover. Having a shower bench or even a bathroom stool on hand helps.

We live in a tech-dominated world where we are constantly connected. Family members, friends, and other well-wishers might be eagerly anticipating a call or message about the baby's arrival. Once the baby and mother are declared healthy and fit, it is time to get on with the phone calls. Start calling up your near and dear to share this good news. Ensure that you do it so your partner can get some rest.

It might seem quite obvious but it is worth mentioning — let your partner sleep as much as she can right now. Taking care of a newborn will be tiring and she needs to recover before doing all that. So, take over with the baby care and let your partner rest until the next feeding session. If you are formula feeding, take over that responsibility so she can rest for longer.

Now, it is time to handle some business. In addition to making an appointment with a lactation consultant, schedule your baby's first pediatric appointment. The pediatrician at the hospital will inform you of the best time frame based on everything going on. All you need to do is make a quick call, let them know the baby is born, and add the appointment to your calendar.

An important part of the business all new fathers must do is add the baby to their insurance. The insurance company will not do this automatically. Companies usually give a period of 30-days within which such inclusions should be made. Do this immediately so it means one less task to complete once the baby is home.

You will also need to fill out your baby's birth certificate. This is the first legal document that formally announces your baby's arrival. This formality is usually completed during the discharge routine. So, ensure that you and your partner have either shortlisted or decided on the baby's name. You will have a day to do this, but the sooner you get it done the better.

Chances are your partner might have been craving foods she wasn't allowed to eat during the pregnancy such as deli meats or sushi. Make her feel better by getting the foods she was craving. Ensure that you encourage her to drink plenty of water. Apart from this, make it a point she is eating foods rich in dietary fiber. This is good for her digestive system.

When Can You Bring Your Baby Home?

If your baby was delivered full term that is after 37-weeks of gestation and is healthy, both mother and baby qualify for a discharge between 24-48 hours after birth. If it was a C-section, your partner might be required to stay in the hospital for up to four days after delivering for observation. Most insurance plans usually cover a 2-day hospital stay for vaginal deliveries and up to a 4-day stay for cesarean births.

Before you can leave, the baby and the mother will need to undergo a couple of tests. A hospital pediatrician will examine the baby and conduct a heel-stick blood test. This helps screen for potential metabolic disorders including phenylketonuria. A hearing screening test will be performed to test the baby's hearing.

An initial physical exam will be conducted on the newborn right after birth to detect any abnormalities, cardiorespiratory disorders, or birth injuries. During the hospital stay, a thorough exam will be performed within the 24-hours of birth. Certain vaccines will also need to be administered to the baby to ensure their overall health and efficient functioning of the immune system. One such vaccine is the hepatitis B vaccination. This offers long-term protection against hepatitis B and is given within 24 hours of birth. Apart from it, either an oral dose or injection of vitamin K is given to promote blood clotting and reduce the risk of serious bleeding.

To ensure that the mother is healing properly, several additional tests will be performed by the medical staff. These usually check whether the uterus is contracting properly and if the bleeding has slowed down or not. She might experience heavy bleeding for a couple of days after a vaginal delivery but it reduces with each subsequent day. It does not go beyond six weeks in case of a normal delivery without any complications.

Basic skills such as successfully breast or bottle-feeding the baby will be checked. Remember, it was mentioned that you need to check with a lactation consultant? This is where it comes in handy. This is to ensure the new mother can perform basic tasks such as caring for the baby, bathing and caring for the umbilical cord stump and changing diapers. These are just some tasks all fathers should learn as well. So, ensure that you are there with your partner while the hospital staff is showing you how to do all the above-mentioned responsibilities.

Before you take the baby home, you will need to sign forms such as a birth certificate, information for a Social Security card, and the discharge form. Even if you have not yet named the baby, you will need to fill out the birth certificate that includes the names of the biological parents.

If you decide to circumcise your baby, get it done during the hospital stay itself. This is a personal choice and a cultural practice. So, it is entirely up to you. It is recommended to complete the procedure as soon as a baby is born and is still in the hospital to reduce the discomfort and promote better healing.

Freebies

Most hospitals usually offer a couple of freebies or samples of postpartum products that are useful for new parents. Each hospital might do it differently but they certainly offer a couple of items discussed here.

Peri Bottle

This is commonly used for cleaning the vaginal area after birth. It helps soothe the skin and heal any tears caused during vaginal birth.

Breast Pump

All new mothers need a breast pump. Anyone who is breastfeeding should have this in their essential supplies. This is even more important, especially if your partner decides to pump exclusively. In such cases, the hospital might send you home with a hospital-grade breast pump.

Donut Pillow

Sitting comfortably can seem like a difficult task after delivering a baby. A donut pillow will make postpartum sitting more comfortable and easier.

Large Maxi Pads and Mesh Underwear

Maxi pads and mesh underwear are by no means attractive, but it's all about comfort for now. These are a lifesaver because your partner will be bleeding quite a bit after delivering the baby. To promote healing and comfort, douse the pads with witch hazel or place them in the freezer.

Breastfeeding Supplies

Breastfeeding may sound quite straightforward, but it is rarely the case. Your partner will need basic breastfeeding supplies such as feeding logs and nipple cream. If your partner is facing any issues with breastfeeding or has doubts about it, ensure she contacts a lactation consultant at the hospital itself.

Newborn Hat, Receiving Blanket, Diapers, and Other Supplies

Your baby will receive a classic hospital hat and this is needed for regulating their body temperature. In addition, you might also receive a blanket, diapers, and other clothing supplies. These supplies will give you a head start on all the different everyday things you will need for your baby.

Baby Bottles and Pacifiers

You can never have too many feeding bottles or pacifiers when you have a baby. So, if your hospital gives any away, take them.

Nasal Aspirator

Removing mucus from a newborn's air pathways becomes easier when you use a nasal aspirator. This is a gentle approach, so you and your partner must learn how to do it.

Formula Samples

Even if your partner decides to breastfeed, having a couple of formula samples on hand can never hurt. If you decide to go the formula route, trying out a few samples helps to determine the ones your baby likes the best. This also comes in handy if your baby is struggling with breastfeeding or is unable to breastfeed due to various reasons.

Bringing Baby Home

After the baby and mother have undergone the required tests and checkups and are declared fit for discharge, it is time to bring them home. This is a moment you both have been waiting for. Your bundle of joy will finally be home. That said, bringing your baby home is also a procedure in itself. Most hospitals and state laws require the installation of a baby seat in a car. The hospital authorities will also check whether the seat is installed before discharge.

You don't have to feel rushed to go home. If you have any questions, worries, or concerns, ensure they are answered and you get the required clarifications before taking them home. It's better to do this at the moment with experts instead of going to bed with the said worries. There is no rush or pressure as there is no compulsion. If it feels like your partner needs another day in observation, let her stay. It is okay.

It's important to dress your baby carefully before taking them home. This is a completely new environment and therefore, you are the best judge. If it is extremely hot, avoid dressing your baby in warm clothes. Dress them how you will dress. If the weather is warm: a light t-shirt, cotton pants, and a baby blanket over their legs will do the trick. On the other hand, if it is cold, ensure the baby has warm clothes: a jacket, hat, mittens, and a warm blanket. To avoid suffocation, keep the blanket away from your baby's face at all times. Keeping them warm is different from wrapping them tight like a burrito.

As mentioned, states require parents to have a car seat for child safety before leaving the hospital. Ensure it is installed before your partner's due date. The infant must never be placed in a rear-facing seat or a convertible seat in the front of the car. The baby safety seat should always be installed in the rear.

Once your baby is home, it brings your partner's pregnancy to an end. That said, the postpartum recovery period has just started. Her body has been through quite a roller coaster ride and she will at least take a couple of weeks to recover. In the meanwhile, ensure you are tending to her needs as well as the baby.

Chapter 2: Helping Mommy Recover

Recovering from the trauma of childbirth is not an overnight process. Remember, she carried the baby in her womb for nine months and it will take some time before she has fully recovered. The recovery period could be even longer, especially if she underwent a c-section. She will experience a variety of physical and emotional changes during the postpartum period, especially the first six weeks after delivery. This is when her body starts healing internally and gets acclimatized to not being pregnant anymore. Most women usually recover within 6-8 weeks of delivering the baby but others might not feel like their pre-pregnancy selves until a few months later. We are all different and so are our bodies. Instead of getting worried or anxious, the best thing you can do right now is learning about the different physical and emotional changes she might experience. Simply learning about postpartum healthcare and what to expect will leave you better prepared to help your partner after her delivery.

Physical Changes

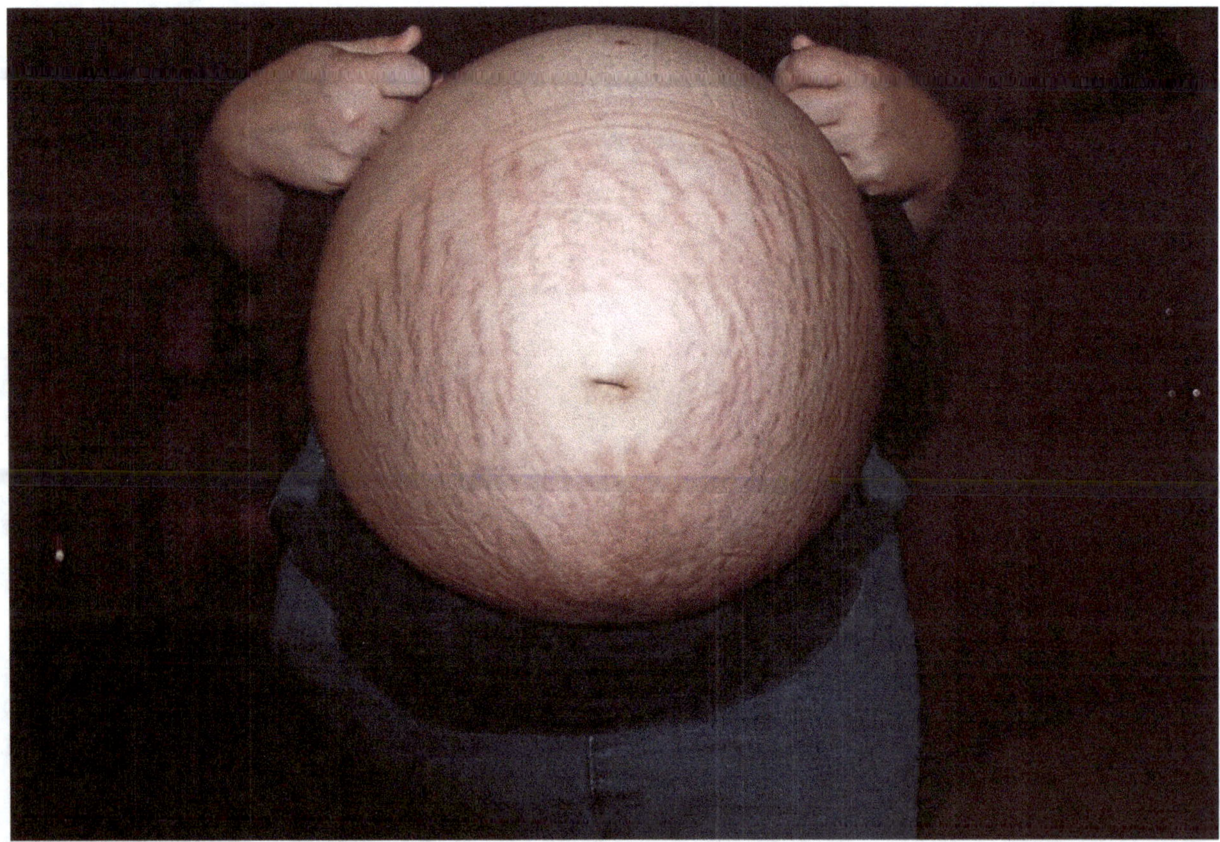

You must pay attention to your partner's physical health, especially during the first six weeks after delivery. Chances are she is extremely tired and too focused on the newborn to think about anything that's happening within her body. Ensure that she does not overexert herself right now because it can harm her recovery. Instead, she needs to nourish her body and stay hydrated, especially if she's breastfeeding. It is most important she gets plenty of rest. So, here are some physical changes your partner will experience during the postpartum period.

Physically Drained and Sore

Your partner's body is going to be physically drained and tired for the next week at least. She not only will be physically tired but sore. During pregnancy, her body expanded to accommodate the growing fetus. After giving birth, it will need to get accustomed to going back to its previous self. This is not an easy process and while she is recovering, she will experience physical pain and tiredness. Depending on whether it was a vaginal delivery or a c-section, the general tiredness and soreness she experiences will vary. That said, during the first one or two weeks of the postpartum period, she will need a good amount of quality rest.

Sore and Engorged Breasts

After childbirth, the mother's body produces colostrum for the next three-four days. It's a nutrient-rich substance essential for strengthening the baby's immunity system. Once the colostrum stops, the breasts will swell up with milk. Pumping or nursing helps reduce tenderness and swelling. Placing a cold washcloth between feedings also helps. While she's not breastfeeding, ensure she wears a firm, soft, and supportive nursing bra.

Vaginal Soreness

During labor, the area between the vagina and anus, known as the perineum, can stretch and tear. If she underwent an episiotomy, where a small surgical incision was made to widen the vagina, the postpartum pain can be further worsened. Episiotomy stitches she receives can take up to six weeks to fully heal. In the meanwhile, placing an ice pack and sitting on a pillow instead of a hard surface helps ease her pain. Apart from this, ensure she presses a clean washcloth or a clean pad against the sore area after bowel movements to ease the pain and avoid infection.

Constipation

Bowel movements will not be easy after delivery. This is a side effect of pain meds given during delivery. She might also be afraid of damaging the episiotomy stitches during bowel movements. The best thing to do right now is to take a prescribed stool softener and consume high-fiber foods that promote bowel activity. Apart from that, she should drink plenty of water and fluids to stay hydrated. Applying witch hazel helps reduce pain and itching that are commonly associated with hemorrhoids.

Hot and Cold Flashes

It is quite common for women to experience hot and cold flashes after pregnancy. This is associated with the hormonal changes her body is undergoing as it is returning to its pre-pregnancy state. Usually, she will stop experiencing them within a week or ten days of giving birth. In the meanwhile, ensure she dresses comfortably, and the temperature in the house is always pleasant and comfortable.

Urinary or Fecal Incontinence

Mild urinary or fecal incontinence is another side effect of delivering a baby. This is because the bladder is stretched during vaginal delivery and results in short-term nerve and muscle damage. This can result in experiencing difficulty urinating even when the urge is strong. Pouring water over the genitals while sitting on the toilet reduces the sting while peeing. Coughing or laughing can also cause urinary incontinence. Simple pelvic floor exercises such as kegel exercises help. Encourage her to tighten her pelvic floor muscles consciously for 5 seconds before relaxing and repeating it 10 times in a row. She must practice kegel exercises up to 10 times daily to strengthen her pelvic floor muscles.

After Pains

Contractions don't end with labor. Some women experience contractions that feel like menstrual cramps or abdominal cramps for a couple of days after delivery. This is because her uterus is shrinking to its pre-pregnancy stage. The cramps can be especially painful when she is nursing the baby because certain chemicals are released in the body causing the uterus to contract. Placing a heating pad on the belly and using an over-the-counter prescription pain reliever should help. That said, ensure you consult her medical practitioner before she uses any medicines right now.

Vaginal Discharge

For the next couple of weeks after delivery, she'll experience vaginal bleeding as well as discharge. Her body is essentially trying to get rid of all the extra tissue created to support the baby during the pregnancy. During the first couple of days, she might notice bleeding that's bright red which slowly turns brownish before becoming yellow and disappearing. During the first 10 days, the discharge can be the heaviest. If the clots expelled are any bigger than a quarter when she bleeds, medical attention is needed. It's recommended she doesn't use tampons and instead opts for sanitary pads for vaginal discharge.

Weight

Her bodyweight will not miraculously go back to its pre-pregnancy level. Instead, it will reduce gradually according to her diet. After delivery, a new mother's weight will be around 12 lbs below her full-term weight. Her body will slowly reduce the additional water weight within the first week or so as it regains its internal balance. To support healthy weight shifts ensure she consumes healthy and wholesome meals.

Emotional Changes

Physical and emotional health are interdependent. While her body is experiencing a variety of physical changes, she will experience emotional changes too. The most common emotional changes you must be mindful of are baby blues and postpartum depression.

Baby Blues

Most new mothers experience a variety of emotions. It might seem as if her emotions are all over the place. She might be extremely happy one moment and irritable, sad or anxious the next. There might also be some unexplainable crying. These symptoms usually subside within the first week or two after delivery. It can be quite confusing for you right now because she might have seemed incredibly excited to bring the baby home and the next minute she's crying.

Remember, if it is confusing for you, it's incredibly confusing and overwhelming for her. All the above-mentioned behaviors are symptoms of baby blues. They refer to the feeling of sadness during the first week of having a baby. They are caused by various hormonal changes and it is not something you should make her feel ashamed about. Instead, be an understanding and supportive partner. You should pay extra attention to her emotional health right now because when baby blues are left unchecked, they can manifest as postpartum depression.

Postpartum depression

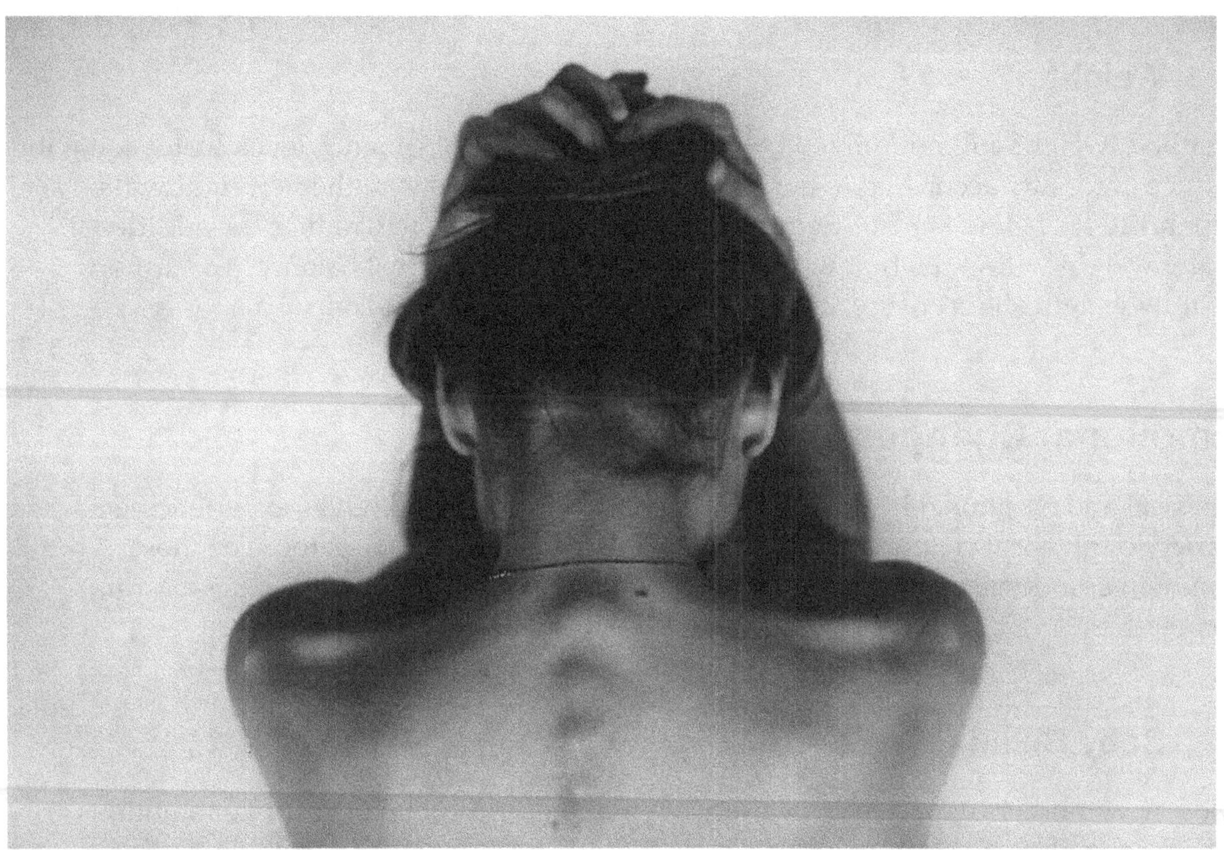

If baby blues become serious or lasts longer than a week or two, she can experience prolonged sadness, severe anxiety and guilt, and even extreme mood swings. All these factors are commonly associated with postpartum depression. Taking care of her emotional wellbeing is as important as her physical health. Chances of postpartum depression increase if there is a family history of depression, she has experienced depression or any other similar mental disorders in the past, or is exposed to a variety of stressors. Right now, you need to be extremely vigilant and sensitive to her mental and emotional needs.

The most common symptoms of postpartum depression you must watch for are:

- A generalized feeling of helplessness, sadness, doubt, or guilt that increases gradually with each passing week
- She has unable to perform basic tasks at home
- She is not able to take care of herself or her newborn
- Drastic changes in her appetite
- She is no longer interested in doing things she once loved
- Harbors serious worries and fears about the baby's well being
- She has no concerns or worries about her baby
- Inexplicable anxiety and panic attacks
- She is constantly worried about harming the baby
- She's scared of being left alone with the baby
- She is experiencing thoughts of self-harm or even suicide

If your partner is showing any of the above-mentioned signs, ensure she gets the professional assistance required. You may even talk to her health care provider; always include her in this conversation. For now, it's important you learn about postpartum depression, make a note of any concerns or questions you have, and discuss them with a professional healthcare provider. You can work along with them and create a list of steps or things that can be done to ensure she feels better. Ensure that you are always accompanying her to her doctor's appointments and let her know that you are there regardless of what happens. For now, do not expose her to any more stress and avoid stressful topics and even decisions until she feels better.

Postpartum Health and Care

Eating

Generally, most new mothers require 1800-2200 calories per day in the month following childbirth. She must consume the minimum calorie requirement. She will also need 500 additional calories while nursing. Remember, she is taking care of the baby and you can do your bit as a conscious partner by catering to her dietary requirements and physical health.

To ensure your partner gets all the important nutrients she lost during the pregnancy, at least half her plate should be filled with fruits, fresh vegetables, and a variety of other fiber-rich foods. The other half must include whole grains such as wheat, barley, oats, quinoa, and so on.

Of course, essential nutrients that should be included in all her meals are protein, calcium, and iron. Ensure that her consumption of processed and prepackaged food is to the bare minimum. Even if it is fruit juices, try to make them at home as much as possible instead of relying on the processed variants. She also doesn't need foods that are rich in added sugars, harmful preservatives, saturated fats, and all other harmful things. If she is nursing, these ingredients will make their way into the baby's system and it is undesirable. Additionally, she may continue the prenatal vitamins if she is breastfeeding. Her doctor might also recommend iron and vitamin C supplements. Ideally, it's advised that nursing women shouldn't consume any caffeine or alcohol. Even if she consumes caffeine, ensure it does not exceed one cup a day.

Exercise

During the postpartum period, exercise or any form of basic physical activity is needed to promote healing. The simplest form of exercise is walking. She might experience some physical discomfort and soreness in the beginning. That said, it is not a reason to avoid exercising. Before she starts doing any exercises, ensure she consults her doctor and is given the clearance to exercise. Core strengthening exercises are also recommended. As mentioned previously, performing kegels helps strengthen the weakened pelvic floor muscles during pregnancy and delivery.

A common and most noticeable physical side effect of pregnancy is stretch marks. Stretch marks usually appear around the abdomen, thighs, and even breasts. Using retinol helps minimize stretch marks. These stretch marks may or may not fade away over time. So, be sensitive to how she feels about them. Ensure that you make her feel loved and cared for. If relevant, taking care of the episiotomy stitches is important too. Ignoring this increases the risk of infections and unnecessary complications. During the first few days after delivery, sitz baths in cold water help. Gradually shift to warm water. Instead of sitting on hard surfaces, place a pillow under her bottom to ease physical discomfort. Using local anesthetic sprays and ice packs further reduces her discomfort and soreness.

If your partner underwent a c-section, the healing and recovery period will be longer. She will be in considerable physical pain during the first couple of days after the surgery. With basic care and rest, this pain will gradually reduce. Ensure that she doesn't take baths and instead receives sponging, doesn't lift weights, and doesn't use the stairs. Apart from this, she should not be driving. If the doctor recommends any other suggestions to promote recovery, make sure she follows them. The c-section's surgical scar must be cleaned with soap and water daily and then dried with a clean towel. Apply an antibiotic ointment to the scar to promote healing.

Postpartum Recovery Checklist

It is important to be fully prepared with supplies to support your partner's mental and physical health. Her postpartum recovery checklist will need the following:

· Acetaminophen or any other pain-relieving medication prescribed by the doctor to soothe overall aches and perineal pain
· Maxi pads, witch hazel pads, ice packs, lidocaine spray, and stool softener for reducing vaginal pain, perineal pain, and hemorrhoids
· Sitz bath for reducing postpartum pain
· Peri bottle to rinse perineal area before and after urinating
· Cotton underwear and nursing bras with nursing pads
· Lanolin and prescription moisturizer to prevent cracked nipples and reduce breast tenderness
· A postpartum recovery belt

When to See a Doctor

Women experience a variety of physical and emotional symptoms during the postpartum period ranging from engorged breasts to baby blues and physical soreness. Most of the symptoms discussed usually reduce on their own within a few weeks. If they don't and you notice or she complains about any of the following, ensure she gets the required medical attention immediately.

· Vaginal bleeding must reduce with each day; if it increases and she is soaking more than one pad every hour
· The size of clots is bigger than a quarter
· Extreme difficulty and pain while urinating
· Vaginal discharge with a strong odor that's not reducing
· Fever of more than 100.4°F and chills
· Spells of dizziness
· Severe and persistent headache and changes to the vision
· Nausea and severe vomiting
· The episiotomy or c-section scar is engorged, red, and swollen with puss
· Gradually worsening abdominal pain and cramps
· Sudden onset of abdominal cramps
· Chest pain, trouble breathing, and heart palpitations
· Extremely swollen or engorged breasts that feel hot to touch and are red
· Increase in general swelling in the body
· Redness and swelling of the legs

How to Help Your Partner Through the Healing Process

You can help your partner through the healing process by being conscious and adhering to the following.

Exercise

If she was used to exercising before and during the pregnancy, she can resume the same once her doctor says it is safe. During the initial weeks of recovery, don't allow her to exercise on her own. The ideal forms of exercise include walking and swimming. This helps restore her strength, promote weight loss, reduce constipation, and increase her energy levels.

Self-Care

Tending to the newborn's every single need will likely become her only priority after delivery. Ensure she doesn't forget about taking care of herself. On a basic level, she must shower daily or at least sponge her body and take naps whenever the baby rests. She shouldn't be following a hectic routine. Right now she needs plenty of time to relax and recover. She should also be granted some time for herself. To do this, you need to help around the house, participate in the household chores and daily responsibilities more than usual. And of course, help her take care of the baby too.

Pitch In

When it comes to taking care of the baby, whether it is feeding, bathing, or changing, participate and help as much as you can. It can be exhausting taking care of a newborn and is doubly exhausting for a new mother. Make it a point to take turns taking care of the little one. For instance, if she is handling the late-night feeding sessions, take charge of the morning feeding time so she can catch up on some sleep.

Try to keep your work schedule flexible and be more hands-on during the weekends. Now is the time to use extra energy to take care of the chores your partner has usually had a responsibility towards for so long.

Take a proactive approach to household chores. Whether it is sterilizing breast pumps, bottles, or pacifiers— do it. Remember, in your attempt to help her don't overburden yourself. There is always the option to hire help, ask family members or friends to pitch in. Try to eat at least one meal with her daily, and you can even cook her favorite meals! You will need to act as a gatekeeper for visitors as well. There will be plenty of well-wishers who might want to pay visits. The first couple of weeks after delivery will be extremely tiring. So, try to limit the guests until she has recovered and limit the duration of their visits too. At times, saying no is the best thing you can do. Also, it is not just your partner who needs to rest. Avoid anything that will overstimulate the newborn too.

It is quite easy for a new mom to feel that all she does is feed or nurse and change the baby. Perhaps any respite she gets from this duty goes toward preparing for the next sessions. In such cases, she might not feel like herself. So, you will need to make a conscious effort to make her feel normal. Whether it is a date night at home or taking over the baby duty so she can go out, do whatever you can to make her feel like herself.

Most new mothers experience a variety of self-image issues. From visible stretch marks to postpartum belly, different things can make her feel unsure of herself. Chances are she probably feels unattractive and is worried about her weight gain. In such instances, you need to help restore her confidence. The simplest way to do this is by dropping a few genuine compliments every now and then. It is not just about making her feel loved, instead, try to make her feel sexy and attractive too! Don't behave as if nothing has changed.

You will find it doesn't take much to surprise your better half. Whether it is a heartfelt note or message, a bouquet, or even her favorite home-cooked meal, express your love. Small and frequent acts of kindness during this period will help strengthen your bond while making her feel special.

Apart from this, ensure that you are 100% present when around her. Be a good listener and be patient. Communicate openly and honestly with each other. Communication is critical for new parents. After all, you both are a team; working together will make you stronger.

From now on, you need to understand and accept the simple fact that your life has changed. It is not just her life, even yours will never be the same. You are now a family of three. At times, this means foregoing weekend golf or game nights. It is okay and you will make your peace with it. Because right now, your wife and baby need you. Prioritize your family and you will see the relationships blossom and thrive.

Stepping into the role of a parent is not only a milestone but an overwhelming change too. That said, you should not ignore your role as a partner. Focusing on your partner's recovery is important but this is not the only thing your new family needs you for. You will also need to spend a lot of your time taking care of the baby which involves holding, feeling, and changing. You will learn more about it in the subsequent chapters. For now, while you are focused on the baby, remember that you cannot forget about tending to your partner's needs.

Chapter 3: Baby Basics — Handling Your Baby

Taking care of your baby is not a responsibility restricted to your partner. New father, it's time that you step up and start doing a little more than your bit when it comes to taking care of the newborn. Even if you have never handled a baby before, you don't have to worry because this chapter includes all the basics you need about handling a baby. From holding one, carrying a baby, and swaddling them to bathing and dressing; everything is covered in detail in this chapter. So, dear dad, you need not get scared because handling a baby is also a skill you can learn within no time.

Holding or Carrying a Baby

You and your spouse understandably might have been incredibly excited to hold your baby. That said, it's important to learn how to hold your baby as well. One of the first things to remember, especially before picking up or holding your baby is to wash your hands. Not just you, anyone who wants to pick up your baby should do the same.

The important neck muscles needed to control and support the head are not yet developed in a baby. Because these muscles are underdeveloped, you need to be extra cautious while holding them. This is also the primary reason why you should place a hand under the head and neck to support them. By the time babies are around 4 months old, they start learning to control and support their head and neck muscles. Even then, you must be extra careful while handling their fontanelles or a soft spot.

While lifting your baby, always place one hand under the bottom and one under the head. Once you have a comfortable grip on your baby, calmly and gently raise their body to your chest level and hold them close to your body.

The most common positions for holding a baby are the cradle hold, belly hold, shoulder hold, and lap hold. You should also pay attention to how the baby is positioned while bottle feeding. The most traditional and common hold most mothers use for breastfeeding is the cradle hold. The baby is essentially cradled on one arm on the same side as the breast of the baby nurses. Hold the baby such that their head rests in the crook of your elbow and their body is turned inward toward your body. Another common hold is the shoulder hold where the baby's body will be parallel to your own and their head rests on your chest and shoulder. Use one hand to support the baby's bottom while the other rests on their head and neck.

Now, if you want to bottle feed your baby, use a cradle hold such that they are in a semi-upright position. The head will be supported by the crook of your elbow while the torso rests along your forearm.

When the baby lies with their stomach resting on their forearm and their head on the elbow, it is known as a belly hold. In this, the baby's feet will land on either side of your hand and that position helps with burping the baby.

For the lap hold, you need to start by sitting in a chair with your feet comfortably placed on the ground. The baby will be placed in your lap such that their head will rest at your knees and they can look up. Use both your hands to lift the baby's head and your forearms must rest under the body. The baby's feet will essentially be tucked in close to your waist.

Since you are now home and may have to be up and about, you can use support items so you are not confined to a specific spot or even a room while taking care of your baby. You can hold them using a sling, carrier, Moses basket, or a bouncer chair so you can prepare food, get on with your chores, or even shower. While doing this, ensure your setups are not around anything that can potentially harm the baby.

If you are scared of holding the baby while standing, start slowly with a seating position. Once you get the hang of supporting their neck and bottom with your hands, you are already there. No need to doubt yourself. While walking up or down the stairs, ensure you are holding the baby in both your arms. Never shake the baby, even if it is to play with them. Throughout your baby's infancy, continue practicing skin-to-skin contact to strengthen your bond.

Your posture is important whenever you are holding or carrying the baby. Ensure that you always carry the baby close to your body and keep your knees bent out. Never carry your baby on the hip. To protect your back whenever you bend over or lift, ensure that you bend your knees. Always straighten your legs as you stand up. Keep your spine straight, engage your core, keep the shoulders back, and maintain this position whenever you are carrying the baby. If you are handing your baby over to others, ideally, ask them to sit. Then gently place your baby in their arms so they are in a basic cradling position. Never hand your baby when you are standing or the receiver is standing.
Remember that newborns don't have a strong immune system. This is one of the reasons why they should be kept away from anyone who seems or is showing symptoms of even cold or flu.

Swaddling a Baby

Swaddling is a technique that's been practiced since time immemorial. This method helps make the baby feel safe and secure. It essentially creates a cozy and warm feeling reminiscent of the time they spent in the womb. In this care method, you will be wrapping your baby and a thin blanket or cloth. This is believed to improve the baby's ability to sleep. Apart from this, it also keeps them warm, especially until their internal thermostat starts working properly.
To swaddle your baby, start by finding a flat surface. Place the blanket on the surface so that they are facing towards you. Gently straighten your baby's left arm, bring up their bottom, and secure the blanket around them. You can also use a ready-made swaddle wrap or a blanket wrap for swaddling. This certainly makes things easier.

While swaddling your baby, you must pay attention to the materials you use are thin and breathable. They should make the baby feel cozy and warm, never suffocated. While swaddling, ensure the bottom of the swaddle is loose enough so the baby's legs are stretched out. This promotes better hip development. To check whether the top of the swaddle is proper or not, fit 2-3 fingers between your baby's chest and the blanket. If you can do this it's wrapped correctly. This gives them sufficient room to breathe without resulting in overheating. Ensure the room temperature is comfortable and not too hot to prevent overheating. Never bundle your baby using extra layers and then swaddle them. This results in heat rash, rapid breathing, flushed skin, and sweating. All these are signs your baby is overheating. As soon as you notice them, remove your baby from the swaddle and undress them.

A swaddled baby should always be put to sleep only on the back and not the stomach. Once your baby starts becoming a little active, knows how to roll over, then you can stop swaddling for just about two months.

Bathing a Baby

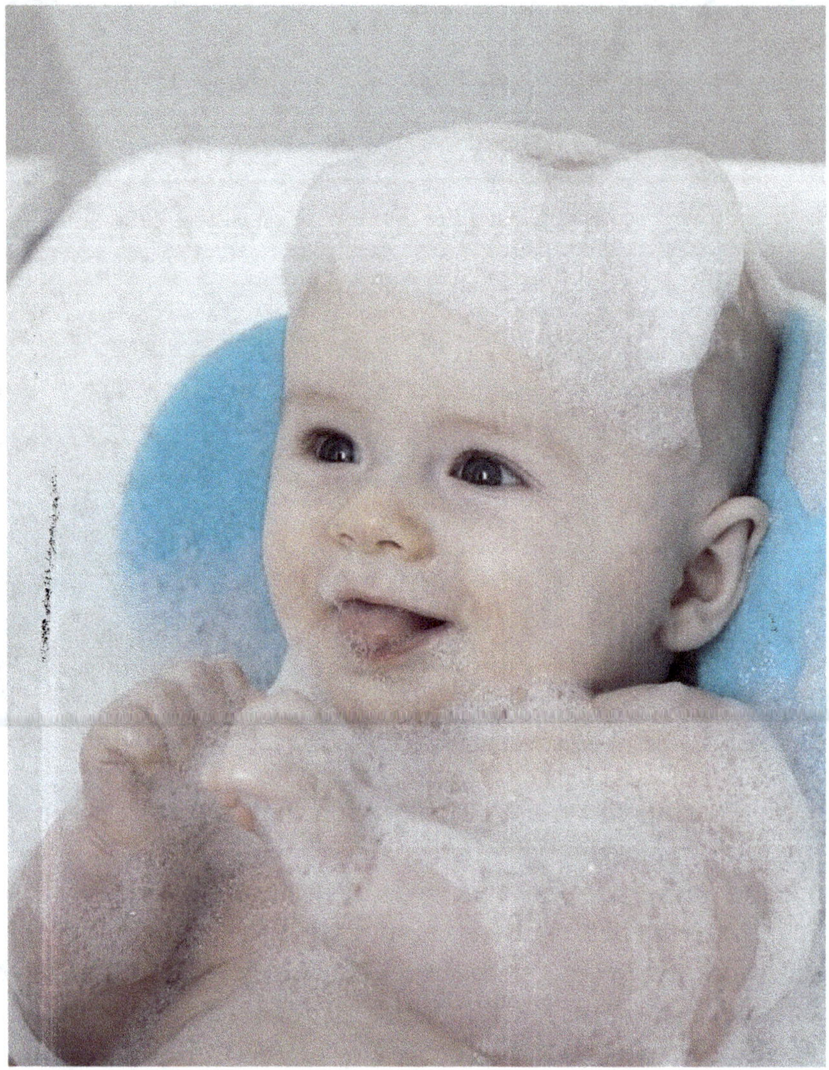

Ideally, a baby's first bath must be delayed until after 24 hours of their birth. The chances of them developing a cold and hypothermia increase if they are bathed immediately after birth. Remember, earlier, it was mentioned that skin-to-skin contact not only strengthens the bond with the mother but is ideal for breastfeeding as well? If the baby is taken away for a bath after birth, this opportunity goes away too. And of course, you don't have to worry about the baby falling ill because a waxy white substance known as vernix covers their skin before birth. This natural substance moisturizes the baby's skin and has natural antibacterial properties.

During the baby's first year, bathe them thrice every week. Frequent baths will dry out the baby's skin. Always use baby wash, soap, and similar baby care products for bathing the baby. Before using any, always talk to your pediatrician. If the baby is hungry or is just done feeding, avoid bathing immediately. Ensure you have all the required supplies before you start bathing them.

Alternatively, you can also opt for a top and tail bath. To do this, simply use cotton wool and warm water to wipe the baby's face and eyes. You can also use a washcloth for the bottom and hands. This helps clean the areas that need awash without giving their entire body a soak. Opting for this reduces the chances of the skin drying up; plus your baby can keep most of the clothes on. While doing this, keep reassuring your baby as you go along and talk to them in a gentle and soothing voice. Additionally use different pieces of cotton wool for wiping their eyes. While washing the baby's hair, you can place them on a table, place your arm under the back, and a hand to cup the head. Then with your free hand, use a gentle hair wash and a washcloth to massage and dry your baby. Don't forget to keep the nappy area clean.

You can give your baby a sponge bath as well. Sponge baths are the safest way to go, baby, until the umbilical cord stem falls away. This also helps if your baby is recently circumcised. You will need to place your baby on a flat surface and ensure they are not on a hard surface. You will need a bowl of warm water, mild baby soap or cleaner, a clean diaper, towel, and washcloth. Ensure the room is warm before you start giving a sponge bath. The ideal temperature is around 75°F. Wrap the baby in a towel after undressing. Unwrap one part at a time while washing the exposed area with a sponge. Start with the face and slowly make your way down the body. Only use warm water and a mild baby wash. The soap-water mixture can be used to clean around the nappy area. Carefully dry the baby so there isn't any moisture between the skin folds.

You can also give the baby a bath in a tub. However, you shouldn't do this until the umbilical cord stump has fallen off on its own. After this, you can slowly submerge the baby's body in the tub. The tub should not be filled with more than 2-3 inches of water. The temperature of the water must not exceed 120°F. While bathing, ensure that you don't forget to support their head using one hand and the other to guide them into the bathtub. Ensure most of their body as well as face is above the water and never leave them unattended even for a second. Your free hand can be used for gently washing and cleaning the body with water and soap. Clean the face, hair, and shampoo scalp using a washcloth. The rest of the body can be washed from the top to bottom using a wet washcloth or warm water. Do all you can to let your baby enjoy bath time.

Now, it's time to dry the baby. It's not just about bathing them, drying them is equally important. While doing this, always ensure you support their head and neck using your hands. Lift them gently out of the bath and place them on a clean, dry, and soft towel on the back. The baby should never be placed on the stomach. Alternatively, you can also place them on the floor and dry the baby on the floor to ensure they don't topple. Dry the baby using a soft towel and don't forget to dry between the creases too. Don't forget to apply zinc paste or any other prescribed ointment to the nappy area if your baby has a nappy rash. Always make the baby wear a diaper before dressing them. Empty the bathwater only after placing your baby in a safe space such as the cot or bassinet.

Dressing a Baby

When it comes to dressing your baby, there are a couple of things you should always remember. The first step is to place the baby on a soft surface so they are comfortable. Don't try holding the baby in your hands or lying down on a table. However, you can place the baby on your lap while stretching the garment's neckline and pulling it over their head. Use your fingers to ensure it does not get caught over the head, face, or ears. It can be quite tempting and feel natural to grab your baby's arm and push through the sleeves; but don't try doing this. Instead, place your hand into the sleeve from the outside and gently pull your baby's arm through the sleeve.

Tips for Dressing

Dressing your baby is a wonderful experience. Once you start buying baby clothes, it becomes extremely difficult to stop. Whenever you are dressing the baby, keep them distracted so it becomes easier. To do this, you can softly talk, sing songs, rhymes, and tell them stories, or even make faces.
While dressing your baby, it's important to pay attention to the weather. For instance, if you are dressing your baby for the cold, you will need to dress them in layers. Always start with a thin layer and start layering over it. This will be the initial layer. Don't forget additional jackets, gloves, or woolen clothes to ensure your baby is covered from head to toe. If you are taking your baby outdoors, you can cover their stroller with a blanket. If the stroller has a rain cover, pull it down.

When it comes to dressing your baby for hot weather, more than 75°F, they just need a single layer of clothing. Opt for light and breathable fabrics. They don't need any mittens or gloves. That said, one accessory that's always important for babies regardless of the weather is a hat. This protects them from exposure to too much sunlight.

How to Select Clothes?

While selecting your baby's clothes, it's not just about looks or comfort that matters, you must always consider material. Opt for soft clothes that fit your baby comfortably and are incredibly easy to take off. The ideal material for baby clothing is good-quality cotton. If there are any buttons or ties on the clothes, ensure they are at the front instead of the back. Diaper changes become much easier if you can snap or strip down both legs. While selecting the clothes, ensure the sleeves are loose fitting so you can push your hands through the shirt to change them by gently grabbing your baby's arm and pulling it out. Look for clothes that are easy to remove, ones that do not have any strings or ribbons that have to be knotted up, wrapped around the baby's neck, or unraveled in any way. These things can become a choking hazard. Certain clothes look quite cute with ribbons and strings and knots, however, you must ensure your baby is always safe.

Avoid tight-fitting clothes, especially ones that have tight bindings around the neck, arms, and legs. Instead, opt for loose-fitting clothes or those made of stretchy fabric. This brings us to a common question most parents have about clothes: How many clothes will the baby need? The answer obviously differs from one parent to another. The answer is, you will need plenty of clothes. You will need at least six onesies, six jumpsuits, two jackets or cardigans if it is winter months, three tops or t-shirts, and two pairs of night dresses or jumpsuits for sleep. Apart from this, you will need three cotton bunny rugs and muslin wraps. You will also need an infant sleeping bag if you don't want to use wraps, a few pairs of socks and gloves, and a couple of hats. Socks and gloves are generally optional and are ideal only for the winter months.

It's not just about dressing your baby, care should be taken while undressing them as well. Once again, it's important to remember you should never pull or tug the clothes off their body. Instead, start by placing your baby on the lap or any other soft surface of your choice. Support your baby's back and head while taking off one sleeve at a time. Gradually stretch the neckline, and then lift it upwards over their chin and face to remove it.

Care must be taken while washing your baby's clothes as well. You must not use any strong detergent or fabric softeners. Remember, the baby's skin is extremely sensitive and softer than adults. So, hard detergents can trigger an allergic reaction.

Bringing Baby Out

This is one part that most parents are usually excited about- taking the baby outdoors. Getting some fresh air is a wonderful way to not just spend time outdoors, but be with your baby as well. Both parents can take turns taking the baby. This situation can be ideal and easy if the baby is completely healthy. That said, a couple of precautions must be taken.

Spending time outdoors is a brilliant way to ensure your baby gets their daily dose of essential vitamin D from sunlight. Spending time under the sun is important, but the type of sunlight your baby is exposed to matters as well. For instance, exposing your baby to the harsh sun at noon and the hours directly after is not advisable. Instead, opt for the early morning's soft and warm sun rays that are pleasant and full of helpful vitamin D. Sunlight exposure is known to promote our mood and energy levels. Even direct sunlight exposure should not exceed 15 minutes. Ensure that you always use sunscreen or a cover if they are going to be spending any longer under the sun.

You must be extremely selective about the outdoor locations you take your baby. Whenever you are taking them outdoors, use your carrier or stroller. Ideally, try to keep your baby as close to your body as possible. Holding them or placing them in a body sling also helps. While using the carrier or the stroller, ensure that the cover is drawn so they are protected from harsh elements, like direct sunlight. Some places that increase your baby's exposure to disease-causing pathogens and other pathogens are schools, hospitals, daycares, airplanes, and doctor's offices. So, whenever possible try to avoid them.

As a rule of thumb, ensure strangers do not touch your baby. Even if they have no visible signs of illness, they can be carriers of harmful pathogens and it increases your baby's chances of exposure to them. Apart from strangers, ensure that other kids keep their hands and faces away from your baby, especially their face, mouth, and hands.

Chapter 4: Baby Basics — All That Goes In

An important decision all parents need to make is about how they want to feed the little one. There are two options here. The first one is to go with the conventional and natural breastfeeding route. The next option is to formula feed the baby. This decision should be entirely left to the mother because ultimately it is her responsibility.

Whether she wants to breastfeed or bottle-feed her baby will depend on her comfort level with breastfeeding as well as her usual lifestyle. Regardless of whether she decides to breast or bottle-feed your baby, the nutritional requirements will be met. So, don't be under any misconceptions that formula-fed babies don't get the required nutrients. Also, do not pressure your partner for breastfeeding if they are not okay with the idea. When it comes to decision-making and her choices for the baby, ensure that you respect your partner's wishes and support what she wants to do.

Now, you must learn about your baby's nutritional requirements and how to cater to them.

Breastfeeding

Apart from a couple of exceptional circumstances, breastfeeding is the best source of nutrition for your baby. For about the first six months, breastfeeding the baby is recommended by the American Academy of Pediatrics (AAP). Different advantages are associated with breastfeeding. The most important one is that breast milk is the perfect food for your baby's underdeveloped digestive system. All the nutrients your baby needs along with its components can be easily digested. Breastfeeding also contains all the proteins and fats your baby requires. Additionally, this creates a stronger bond between the mother and infant.

Another advantage of breastmilk is the helpful health benefits for your partner as well. Nursing makes it easier for new mothers to get back in shape, reduce the risk of breast cancer and even ovarian cancer. It is also quicker when compared to formula feeding because no preparation is required. There are no real chances of running out of breast milk in the middle of the night because her body will keep producing the milk the infant needs. The skin-to-skin contact offered by nursing enhances the emotional connection between mothers and their infants.

Breastmilk is rich with various antibodies that protect babies from respiratory infections, illnesses, and even diarrhea; while reducing the chances of the baby becoming obese or overweight. If your baby is breastfed, they will not need any juices, fluids, or even water during the first six months.

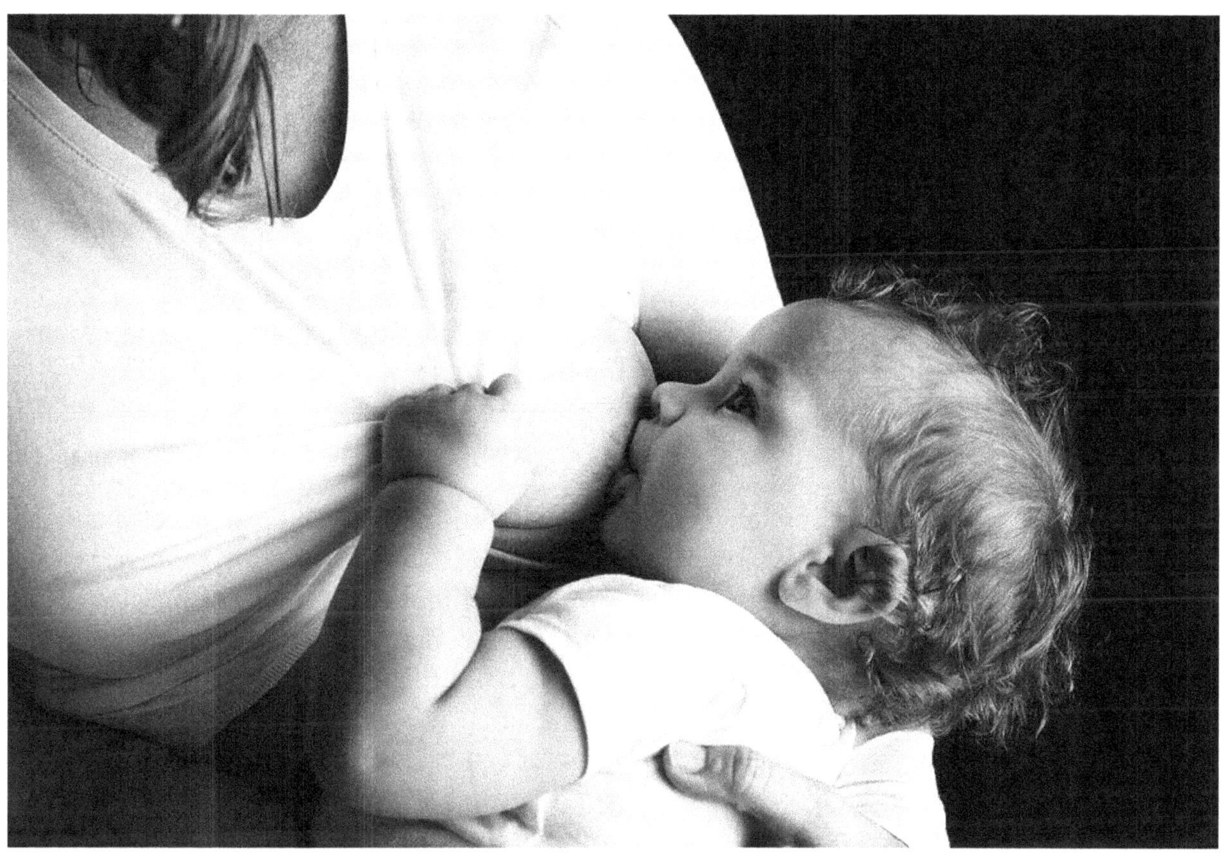

When it comes to breastfeeding, if your partner desires to, she can resume her work and other activities as usual by using a breast pump. Breastmilk can be collected and stored. If you are breastfeeding, ensure that you don't use any pacifiers. Using pacifiers can confuse the baby between a nipple and the pacifier's tip, which can make breastfeeding trickier too.

A common question most new fathers have is how can they become a part of the breastfeeding routine? Doing this is easier than you probably think. For instance, you can carry the newborn to your partner for breastfeeding. Similarly, you can also burp and change the baby after they have been nursed. If your partner is pumping breast milk you can feed the baby or otherwise keep them engaged. If your partner needs anything while breastfeeding, ensure that you cater to her needs. Apart from this, you can also do other things for improving her body's ability to produce breast milk. You can bake lactation cookies or even make mother's milk tea to achieve the goal. Remember, taking care of your baby is not your partner's responsibility alone. It is a team effort, and therefore, you need to take an active role in it.

Bottle Feeding

Even If you are breastfeeding your infant, it's important to understand what bottle feeding is, how it works, and what to avoid while doing it. A nutritious alternative to breast milk is a commercially prepared formula for infants. This means new mothers have greater flexibility and freedom to resume their pre-pregnancy routine. In bottle feeding, you also get a chance to monitor your baby's food intake. The number of feedings a bottle-fed baby needs is smaller when compared to a breast-fed one. The baby's body takes a while longer to digest formula and therefore, they need fewer feedings. Formula-feeding makes it easier to feed in public or when you are on the move as well. Additionally, other family members can take an active part in the feeding sessions giving them more chances for bonding.

When it comes to formula feeding, ensure that you carefully follow all the directions printed on the labels to prepare the formula. Apart from it, do the research required to find a formula that meets your baby's needs and requirements. When in doubt, don't hesitate to reach out to your pediatrician or doctor for a consultation and to get their suggestions and advice before deciding on a specific baby formula.

If you opt to formula-feed, ensure you don't give your baby any fluids other than the formula. Similarly, as stated previously your baby doesn't need anything other than breastmilk if your partner decides to opt for breastfeeding. Until your baby is at least six months old, they don't need other fluids.; meaning you should not give them any juices, water, and even cow and vegan alternative milk. When your baby is 6-months old, you can slowly start introducing water to their diet regardless of whether they are breast or formula-fed.

While preparing the formula, ensure that you don't store it in the refrigerator for longer than 24-hours. The formula needs to be slightly warm, but not hot whenever you are feeding. Before feeding, squirt a little of the formula onto your wrist to check whether it's warm enough or not. Never warm formula in a microwave because it not only results in uneven heating but creates hotspots that can burn your baby's mouth.

If you are feeding with a bottle, ensure you are sitting comfortably in a chair or glider while the baby is placed in your arms. Your feet must be firmly planted on the ground while the baby is held in a cradle hold. Don't feed the baby when they are lying flat on their back because it increases the risk of choking. Apart from it, never let the baby fall asleep with a bottle in the mouth; this increases the risk of ear infections and even tooth decay.

A wonderful thing about bottle feeding is it gives fathers and other family members a chance to take an active part in the baby's feeding routine. You can easily take over all the feeding sessions when home if you are bottle-feeding the baby. This gives the new mother a break to do other things. You can also take on the responsibility of thoroughly sanitizing and cleaning the feeding bottles, making them ready for the next feeding.
If your baby is vomiting right after feeding, it could be a sign of an allergy or some type of digestive trouble. It might also be due to an underlying infection or condition that requires immediate medical attention. If this pattern continues, consult the pediatrician right away.

How Often Do Newborns Feed?

The feeding requirements of newborns are different. Every baby is unique but one pretty consistent thing is bottle-fed babies need fewer feeds than breastfed ones. Breast milk is easier for the baby's body to digest and therefore, they will need more frequent feeds. Ideally, it's recommended that mothers should nurse their babies one hour after birth. After this, for the first couple of weeks of their life, they will need anywhere between 8-12 feedings when breastfed. Of course, there is no rest for the weary, and this is something all new parents know. During the initial stages, your partner should try nursing your baby for 10-15 minutes on each breast. After this, the period can be adjusted as required. Usually, babies eat once every 1-3 hours, and breastfeeding should always be on-demand. The duration between the feeds increases while the frequency reduces as the baby grows. It is recommended that a newborn should not go without feeding for longer than 4-5 hours at a stretch.

So, how can parents determine when their baby needs to be fed? The most common sign a baby is hungry is when they start moving their head from one side to another while opening and closing their mouths. Another sign is when they stick out their tongues and pucker their lips to make a sucking motion. If a baby places their fists or hands in their mouth or nuzzles their mother's breasts, it is a sign of hunger. Another sign you cannot ignore is when the baby starts crying incessantly.

On the other hand, you should look for signs when your baby is full. Overfeeding increases the chances of your baby vomiting. If your baby voluntarily pulls away from the bottle, breast, or spoon or refuses to take it to them, it is a sign they are full. If your baby falls asleep while feeding or hands the food back to the feeder, it means their tiny tummy is full. If babies tightly close their mouths and refuse to open them or keep shaking their heads from side to side, it shows they are full.

Supplements

Almost all breastfed babies need a vitamin D supplement, especially during the first couple of days of their life. They will need additional vitamin D until they are at least a year old. Their daily dose of this can be obtained in the form of formula fortified with vitamin D. Even iron-fortified supplements are usually recommended because they contain the right blend of vitamins and minerals. Before you even think about adding any supplements to your baby's diet, ensure you consult their pediatrician. Without the pediatrician's guidance or advice, never give your baby any form of supplements.

Burp Your Baby

When it comes to taking care of your baby, there is another important step after feeding; you should also learn to burp them. This is quite important because it helps eliminate excess air that babies usually swallow while feeding. If you are burping a baby, always place a bib or a towel under their chin or on your shoulder. This prevents clean-up, especially when your baby spits up or has a wet burp.

The position is crucial when you are burping the baby. The ideal position is to hold them upright while their head rests on your shoulder. Don't forget to use your hand to support their head and back. With the other hand gently pat on their back until they burp. Another position you can use is to sit comfortably on a chair while the baby sits on your lap. We use one hand to support their head, chin, and chest while the other is used to gently pat their back. The third option is to lay the baby down on their tummy on your lap. Their head must be placed such that it's higher than their chest and you are holding onto it. Your free hand should be used for gently rubbing or patting the baby's back until they burp.

The ideal time to burp the baby is once they have had 2-3 ounces of bottle-feeding or formula. Alternatively, burp them every time they switch from one breast to another when the mother nurses. After your baby is fed, ensure they are kept upright for at least 10-15 minutes to ensure the milk does not come back up. If your baby usually spits up or has an acid reflux condition, you might need to hold them in this position for a while longer.

One condition you need to prepare yourself for is when babies are not big burpers. Some don't burp as much as others and that's perfectly alright. As long as this does not get in the way of other activities of your baby, it's nothing to worry about. The digestive system of a baby also matures as they grow, so burping them can become unnecessary after some time. Usually, this takes about 4-6 months or around the time when the baby starts eating solid foods.

Solid Foods

Until the baby is six months old, don't introduce any solid foods. At this time the baby will ideally be about 13lbs and be able to hold its head up. Introduce these solid foods once the baby is 6-12 months old. Always start with soft and easy-to-swallow foods such as one-grain cereals, pureed fruits and vegetables, and mashed foods. You can introduce well-chopped finger foods too. While starting solids, introduce only one food at once and wait for at least 3-4 days before introducing another. This allows you to notice any allergies or reactions the baby might have to certain foods. Babies between 6-12 months will need formula or breastmilk along with solid foods.

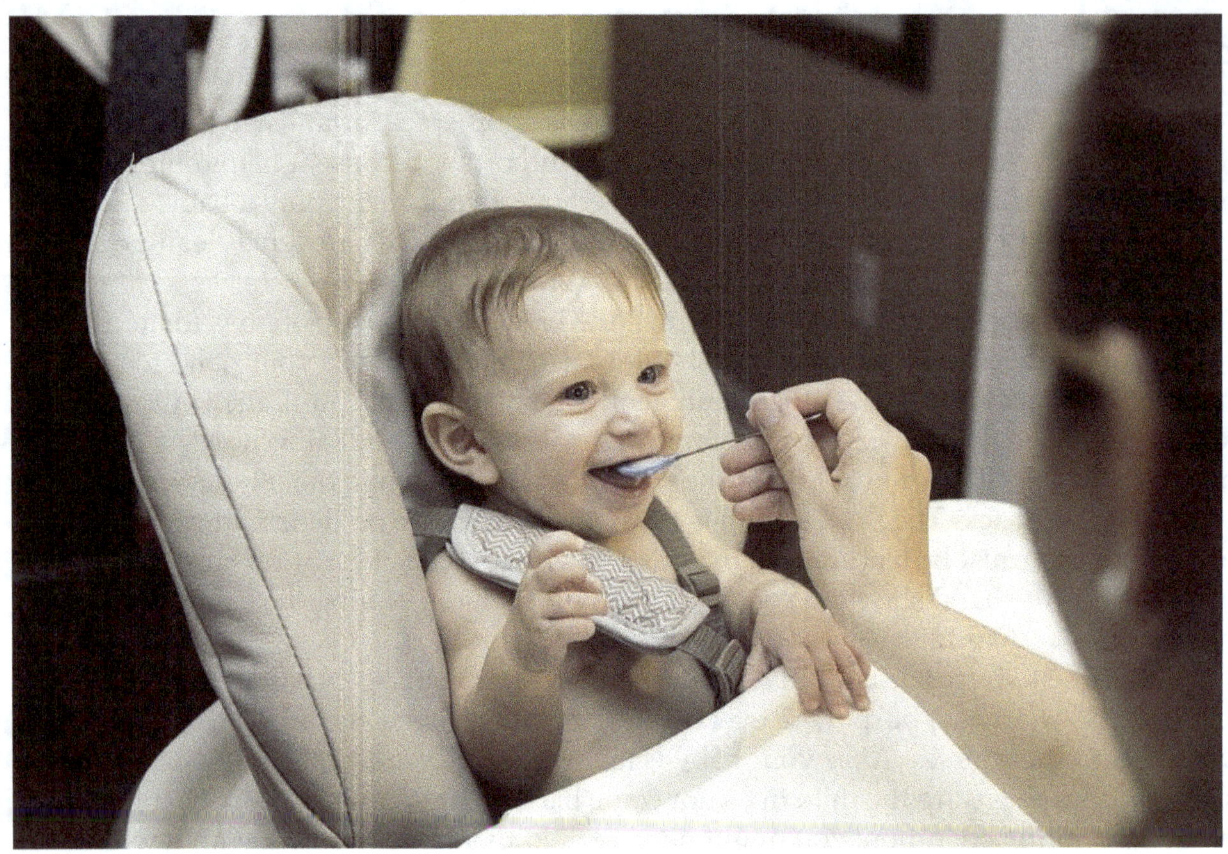

If the baby is exclusively breastfed, they will need solid nourishment between 4-6 months. Some common signs your baby is developmentally ready to start eating solid foods is when they can sit upright with hardly any support, can control their head for prolonged periods, are interested in whatever you are eating, and start readily opening their mouths to accept food from a spoon. Apart from this, if the baby seems hungry despite 8-10 feedings of breast milk or approximately 32 oz formula, it means they are ready for solid foods. Before starting solid foods, don't forget to consult your pediatrician.

When it comes to feeding solids, you can opt for poultry, fish, meat, vegetables, and different colored fruits. When compared to fruits and cereals, meats and vegetables have more nutrients in a single serving and are, therefore, ideal for babies. If you decide to make baby food at home, using pureed corn, sweet potatoes, peas, and potatoes is recommended. Don't use any flavorings including salt and sugar until your baby is at least one year old. Usually, it's suggested babies should not be fed homemade purees containing spinach, green beans, carrots, and squash; however, the commercial variants are okay to a certain extent. Any food that is a potential choking hazard such as big chunks of vegetables is never ideal. Babies are still learning how to chew slowly and therefore, have increased the risk of choking. Similarly, avoid foods that can upset your baby's stomach, such as ones filled with sugar, spices, and salt.

The baby's water intake must increase once you start introducing them to solid foods. Most infants usually eat anywhere between 3-6 times including meals and snacks.

Chapter 5: Baby Basics — All That Comes Out

Fatherhood is certainly not rocket science, but it is not the easiest thing to do in the world. Apart from feeding and taking care of your baby, it is important to understand their excretions as well. It certainly might not be an interesting or cutest topic, but it is extremely important. Learning about all that comes out of your baby teaches a lot about their general health. The excretions you need to pay attention to spit up, vomit, pee, and poop. You need to learn how to change diapers, understand what different poops signify, deal with diaper rash, and learn to take care of your baby when they are vomiting.

Vomiting and Spitting Up

The most common sign of any illness or even infection in your baby is vomiting or spitting up. That said, seeing your baby do either of these things can trigger a bout of anxiety. Instead of feeling helpless or anxious, learning about what causes them and how you can prevent or help your baby is the best course of action.

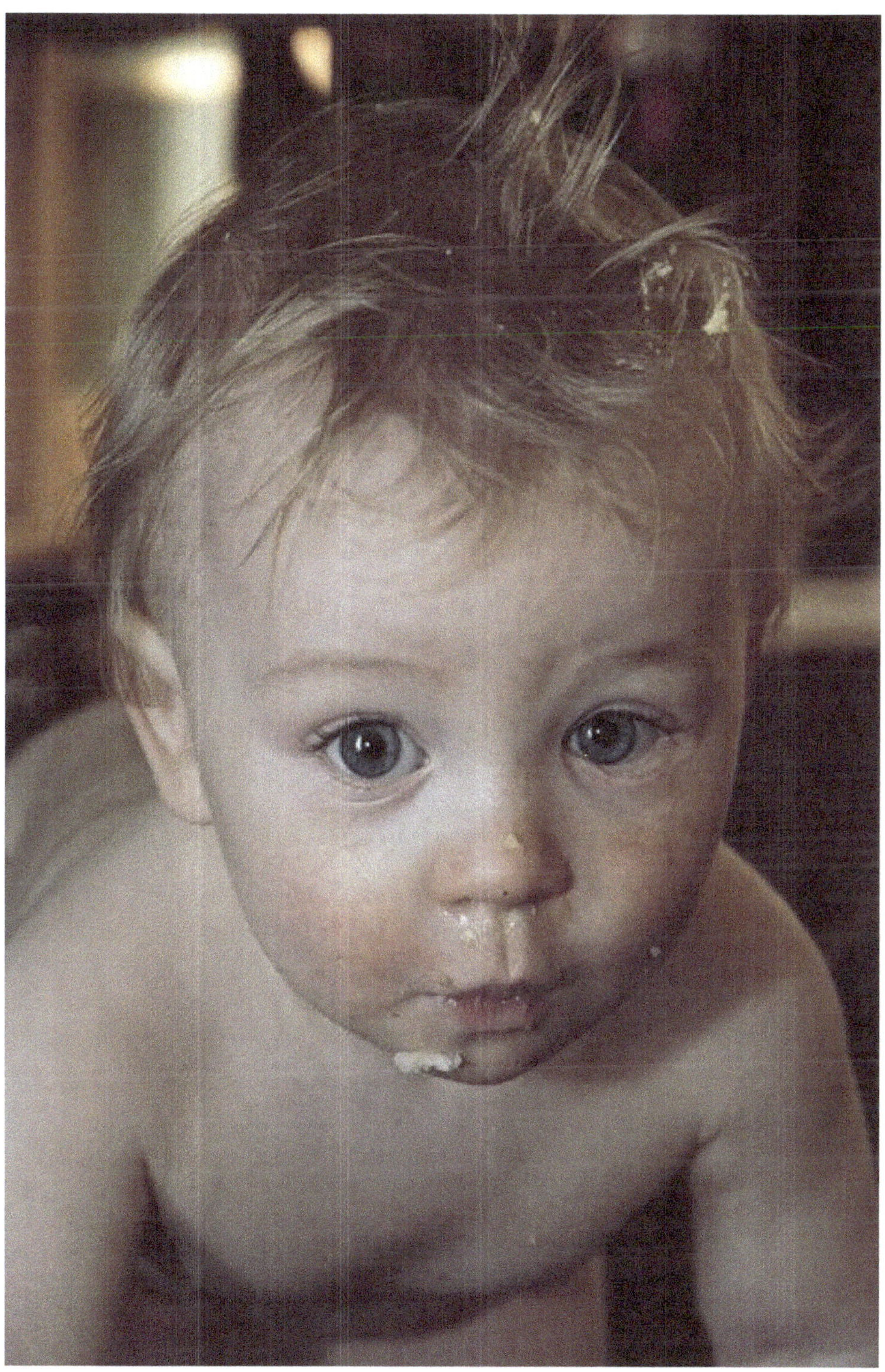

The first step is to understand there is a difference between vomiting and spitting up. When the stomach contents are forcefully thrown up through the mouth it's known as vomiting. On the other hand, the easy flow of stomach contents from the mouth during the early years of infancy is known as spitting up. This usually happens when the baby burps or even hiccups. The abdominal muscles along with the diaphragm vigorously contract and the stomach stays relaxed during vomitings.

Spitting up is quite common in healthy babies. Most babies are usually happy spitters and that means, they don't have any breathing troubles, sleep well, and are comfortable. Usually, spitting up in babies stops by the time they are about 4 months old. If you want to reduce spit-up, start burping your baby more frequently, ensure you do not overfeed them in one go, and never engage them in any physical activity after feeding. You should also ensure your baby stays in an upright position for at least 30 minutes after feeding. Whenever they are eating, make sure there isn't any extra pressure on the stomach area. You can also try a different formula to see what works. Apart from this, if you notice they are spitting up despite avoiding all the above-mentioned things, ensure you change the diet. For instance, the consumption of excess dairy can increase the chances of spitting up.

If you notice any of the following, contact your pediatrician immediately. These can be a sign of an underlying problem or even an illness.

- The spit-up is green or yellow, has blood in it, or any material that looks like coffee grounds.
- Your baby is not gaining any weight.
- Your baby has breathing problems and/or difficulty breathing.
- Your baby has diarrhea and/or a fever.

As with spitting up, vomiting is also quite common during the early phase of infancy. During the first month of your baby's birth, vomiting will be quite common and you don't have to worry. It is usually a sign of slight feeding difficulty, however persistent vomiting can be a sign of something else altogether. If your baby is vomiting constantly, it could be a sign of obstruction in the intestines, infection, allergy to protein, or even gastroesophageal reflux disease (GERD).

If you notice any of the following, please contact the pediatrician immediately regardless of your baby's age.

- The baby is vomiting for more than 24 hours, is unable to drink sufficient fluids, and has signs of dehydration.
- The abdominal region looks swollen or enlarged and is accompanied by abdominal pains and convulsions as well.
- The vomit is green-colored or has blood in it.

Peeing and Pooping

Anything that goes into the body needs to come out. This concept takes on a completely different meaning when you have a baby. Chances are, your baby is constantly peeing, pooping, vomiting, or spitting up. When you keep looking at everything that goes out from their tiny body, it will leave you wondering if there is anything left within the system or not. To ensure your baby is not malnourished, you will need to start inspecting their diaper contents. This is an activity most new parents do with zeal unlike any other. The number of bowel movements a newborn has gradually increased over the first week of their life. The bowel movement also depends on the quantity of formula or breast milk they are consuming. During the first week, expect at least 10 diaper changes every day. This is, however, not a strict rule or a guideline. For instance, on the first day, there might just be one dirty diaper, on the second there will be two dirty diapers, on the third will be three, and so on. This goes on until the 5th or the 6th day.

Your baby might want to be fed once every two hours or once every 4-6 hours. This feeding is once again associated with their internal workings and whether they are consuming breastmilk or formula. Usually, any baby who is breastfeeding can have anywhere between 1-12 small stools daily. Your baby will have at least 1 bowel movement per day if they are formula-fed. Don't forget to change the baby's diaper whenever they have a bowel movement. Once they have crossed the newborn stage, breastfed babies might have a bowel movement once every four or five days.

Dear parent, do not panic because an infrequent bowel movement at this stage is not a sign of constipation. As long as your baby's stools are soft and their overall behavior is normal, it is not a problem or concern. Your baby is not constipated if they are nursing normally, are gaining weight steadily, and seem normal in general. If all this seems regular they are generally healthy.

Never self-medicate your baby based on what others seem to be doing. Always consult your pediatrician before administering any form of treatment to your little one. This means you should not give any enemas or suppositories because you believe your baby is constipated. Their digestive system is quite different from an adult's and going a couple of days without having a bowel movement is not uncommon.

You might have seen most new parents excitedly tracking their baby's pee and poop. It's quite similar to how trackers track pugmarks and examine the animal fecal matter in the wild. Well, it is time for you to become an enthusiastic tracker and understand what your baby's pee and poop mean. You can learn a lot about their health and well-being by understanding everything that comes out of their system.

Your baby's digestive system will take a couple of days until it gets a jump start. As noted this also depends on whether your baby is relying on formula or breast milk. While breastfeeding, until the mother's milk is fully produced, the baby will not start wetting the diaper as expected. Usually, the baby will pee at least five times daily after the first couple of days. If the urine output does not increase, ensure that you consult a pediatrician immediately. In healthy babies, the pee will be light yellow to dark yellow. During the first week, you might notice brick red or slightly pinkish stains on the diaper. Don't be alarmed when you look at it because it's not blood. Instead, it is just highly concentrated urine. You don't have to worry if your baby is wetting at least four diapers daily.

Now, let's get down to deciphering what your baby's poop means. There are three common types of stools newborns pass: the meconium stage, the transitional stool stage, and the newborn stool stage. During the first 24 hours of life, about 95% of babies poo and pee for the first time. The first bowel movement your baby has is known as meconium. This is the first poop passed by the newborn and it looks like a black and sticky tar. The color of the poop gradually changes from black and moves to greenish-brown. After this, it takes on a hue quite similar to that of mustard. These colors are quite common with breastfed babies. There are no hard and fast rules about the number of bowel movements a baby should have. Some might poop up to 7 times a day while others have a movement only once every seven days. As long as your baby is not showing any other negative symptoms and is healthy overall, you don't have to worry.

Until your baby starts consuming solid foods, their stool will be soft and almost clay-like. The color usually varies between shades of yellow or tan when they are formula-fed. A formula-fed baby's poop is firmer than a breastfed one, but it should never be firmer than soft clay. Don't be alarmed if you notice any green stools as this coloring is quite common.

If your baby's stools are very dry or hard, it means they are not getting sufficient fluids or have an infection. When compared to formula milk, breast milk hardly leaves any residue for the body to be eliminated. So, the frequency of the stools is not usually associated with constipation and isn't a problem as long as the overall stool is soft and loose. If the baby is formula-fed and does not have at least one bowel movement daily, it can be a sign of constipation. If your baby is not pooping or peeing as regularly as they started or are supposed to, do not hesitate to immediately consult their pediatrician.

Diaper Duty

Diaper duty is not glamorous, but learning when to change, how to change them, and how to dispose of them is important information. After all, if your partner is resting, dealing with all this will be your responsibility. Let us start with the most important part of diaper duty; which is changing the diaper.

You can opt for either cloth or disposable diapers. Each has its pros and cons. Cloth diapers are environmentally friendly, but cleaning and sterilizing them is quite an elaborate process. Cloth diapers need to be changed more frequently too. To wash the cloth diapers, you need hot water mixed with a mild detergent. Avoid adding fabric softeners while washing diapers. Remember, you should only use mild detergent because the baby's skin is extremely sensitive right now. On the other hand, disposable diapers are incredibly convenient and easy to use.

Another question that most parents wonder about is when they need to change the diaper. The obvious answer might be to change it as soon as the baby pees or poops in them. Well, you should never let a baby stay in a dirty or bad diaper for too long either. It not only increases the risk of diaper rash but infections as well. As soon as the diaper is wet, you need to change it. If the diaper is soiled, change it within the hour to prevent any irritation. If your baby has a bowel movement, ensure the soiled diaper is changed right away. An ideal time to change the diaper during the middle of the night is whenever the baby wakes up to feed or has soiled their diaper.

Always keep a towel handy while changing a diaper. If you are changing a boy's diaper, always create a shield with the front of the diaper. On the other hand, if you are changing a girl child, always wipe from front to back. Ensure that there is no fecal matter around the genital area.

An important aspect of taking care of your baby's diaper region is to watch out for diaper rash. These are extremely common and can be a source of extreme discomfort for your bundle of joy. They usually start appearing as localized redness on the buttocks or the genital region. They might also start as small reddish bumps. If you notice these bumps, it's the first sign of a diaper rash. Skin sensitivity, chaffing of skin, staying in wet diapers for long periods, or infrequently changing diapers are the most common causes of a diaper rash. Using sufficient ointment to treat diaper rash is commonly recommended. Usually, the rash goes away within 2-3 days; if it does not subside, consult a pediatrician immediately.

Apart from an ointment rich in zinc oxide, you can also use baby powder. Ensure you always keep the powder away from your baby's face. Similarly, anti-fungal cream, oral antibiotics, or topical antibiotics can be used as well. Always wash your hands before and after changing the baby's diaper. Change the diapers often and as quickly as you can when it gets wet or soiled. Clean your baby's diaper area using a mild cleanser and water. Don't forget to pat the area completely dry using a clean towel instead of wiping or rubbing the sensitive region. Before you put on a new diaper, ensure the area is thoroughly clean and dry.

It's not just important to make your baby wear or change a diaper, disposing of them is equally important. Unfortunately, most parents don't think about it. There are different methods of disposing of depending on if you use disposable or cloth diapers. If you are using cloth diapers, dump the stool in the toilet and then throw it for a wash. Only opt for absorbent and lightweight cloth diapers that are soft instead of the bulky variants. While washing cloth diapers, opt for a mild detergent and hot water instead of a fabric softener. If you are using disposable diapers, wrap the dirty diapers up in paper or keep a bin dedicated to dirty diapers. Ensure you don't let the dirty old used diapers gather, because it is extremely unhygienic.

Now, another important aspect of diaper duty is to pack the diaper bag. This comes in handy whenever you are traveling with your baby or taking them out. The basic things that should be included in the diaper bag are, of course, diapers. Additionally, you'll need an extra change of clothes, a burping rug or cloth, and plenty of gentle wipes. You will need a changing pad and mild hand sanitizer. Don't forget to carry an extra top or shirt for yourself and your partner because the chances of baby vomiting or spitting up are quite high during the first year. You will also need to add some toys your baby likes and books to keep them engaged.

If you are using cloth diapers, ensure you pack an extra bag for holding the soiled or wet ones when you are out. If you are formula feeding, don't forget to carry feeding bottles, formula, and a water bottle too. Even if you are breastfeeding, ensure you carry a feeding bottle filled with breast milk whenever you take your little one out.

Chapter 6: Baby Basics — Calming Baby Down

Babies don't yet know how to communicate. Communication is something even most adults struggle with, so expecting it from a baby is unrealistic. Crying is synonymous with babies. This is the only way through which they can communicate. One thing all parents must quickly understand and learn is what to do whenever the baby acts up. Calming or soothing a baby is not only important for their well-being but your mental peace as well. If you don't want to be left clueless the minute your baby starts crying, here are some suggestions you can use.

Remember, there is nothing unusual about crying. It's problematic when the crying is incessant, and it doesn't go away regardless of everything you do. Babies cry and you need to prepare yourself for it. In fact, during the first 6 weeks of their life, they might cry for 2-3 hours daily. This is common and it usually eases off as they grow.

As you get accustomed to your baby, you will start understanding what each type of cry is about. For instance, your baby's cry when hungry will be quite different from the one when they are sleepy. The simplest way to understand why the baby is crying is to pay attention to their signals. Whenever your baby cries, pay attention to the pitch, noise level, and intensity. Make a note of their facial expressions and body language as well. Even though crying is reasonable, normal, and expected, understanding what exactly normal means is not easy for first-time parents. Whenever your baby cries, the one thing you must not do is get worked up. Remember you need to stay calm if you want to soothe your baby. If you get worked up, it can increase the baby's negative mood and behavior which worsens the situation.

Reasons Why Babies Cry

Before you learn how to calm or soothe the baby, it's important to understand the common reasons why they cry. Perhaps the most common reason why babies cry is that they are hungry, sleepy, tired, or need the diaper changed. If your baby needs to burp and is experiencing stomach trouble such as gas, they will cry. Another reason they cry is that they want to be held. These reasons may seem quite obvious but remember that your baby cannot communicate with words or actions. Crying is their only form of communication. They will even cry if the room is too hot or cold. These general discomforts should be checked first when the baby is crying. If babies are in any physical pain, they usually point or hold the area that troubles them. One common physical discomfort that causes the baby to cry is teething pain. This usually happens between 4-7 months. At times, it can happen even sooner. Regardless of their crying, this is quite uncomfortable for the babies, and you might need to talk to the pediatrician about what's to be done. The simplest way to determine whether it's teething pain or not is by feeling the gums with your finger. If you notice anything bumpy under the skin, it is a sign of teething.

At times, babies cry because something external is hurting them, but the reason can be difficult to notice. In such instances, check for any clothing tags or fabric that is itching or annoying your baby. Similarly, look for any hair tourniquet on your baby's finger or toes ambiance causing their discomfort. Another reason could be the discomfort caused by an uncomfortable position. If this is the reason, simply change the position and the crying should stop.

When babies are under or overstimulated, they start crying. Swaddling helps calm the baby if they are overstimulated. Alternatively, you can place them in a quieter spot or dim the lights to reduce stimulating their senses. On the other hand, if they are understimulated, engage in more activities that help interact with the baby. You can also place them in a carrier and carry them around so they can see what's going on.

Of course, babies usually cry when unwell. If you have eliminated all the reasons mentioned until now, their crying could be a sign of an underlying health problem. Please consult a pediatrician immediately so you can begin to get your baby the support needed.

Calming or Soothing a Crying Baby

Once you have determined that your baby is not crying for obvious reasons such as hunger, infection, a dirty diaper, or any other problems, it's time to calm them. The simplest way to calm the baby is by swaddling them. Swaddling makes them feel comfortable, safe, and secure. Swaddling naturally has an overall calming effect. During the initial stages, non-nutritive sucking also helps. In this, the baby usually sucks on their thumb, fist, or finger. If not, you can also offer your finger or a pacifier. Ensure this does not become a habit and is used only occasionally.

Hold the baby in your arms and gently sway or rock them. Gently stroke their abdominal region or stroke them from the forehead to the back of the neck. Stroking the body gently also has a calming effect. Apart from this, playing a song, soothing music, or singing a lullaby can help. A white noise machine or any other machine that produces white noise such as a clothes dryer, hairdryer, and vacuum cleaner also creates a soothing ambience. A gentle massage or gently bouncing the baby in your arms is a good idea too. The idea is to calm your baby physically so they relax mentally.

If colic is the reason for your baby's crying, a basic cradle hold helps calm and relax the baby. Cradle your baby's head in the arm while laying them on its back. The other hand can be used for stabilizing them while rubbing their back gently. Alternatively, place the baby on a flat surface on their back. Gently move their knees up to their tummy in a motion similar to pedaling a bicycle and hold this position for 10 seconds. Release the position and repeat it a couple of times. You can also hold the baby on the side of the stomach for a different soothing effect.

If you want to calm your baby, carrying them outside and changing the usual environment they are looking at may help. A change of scenery can be calming, but also peacefully stimulating for the baby.

If the baby is crying, you must understand there's a difference between regular crying and colic crying. Colic is a condition where an otherwise healthy baby cries incessantly and inconsolably for over 3 hours at a stretch more than three days a week and at least for 3 weeks.

If your baby's crying feels more like screaming than actual crying, it can be a sign of colic. Colic crying usually occurs late in the afternoon or early evening and goes on for at least a couple of hours. It is caused by deregulation of stress, caused by general fussiness and distress. Hold your baby close to your body and breathe slowly and deeply. By regulating your breathing and calmly breathing, you encourage the baby to do the same. It can be soothing for them. Alternatively, hold the baby as close to your body as you possibly can while rocking them in your arms. They can also be placed in a carrier so they are held close to your body. Close contact helps calm a colic baby.

Keep Calm When the Baby Cries

The most important thing all parents should do is ensure they are calm whenever the baby cries. It is quite normal to feel frustrated whenever your baby cries. But remember, you are dealing with a baby, and learning to deal with crying is a part of the job description. The best thing you can do to avoid getting overwhelmed or feeling extremely frustrated is to ease your burden. Ease the stress by asking someone else to step in and help calm the baby. For instance, if you are frustrated, your partner can take care of the crying baby or maybe your parents, the household members, or even the nanny. Regardless of how frustrated, irritated, tired, or annoyed you are, keep these emotions away from the baby. Your baby is not responsible for any of them. In the end, no one is responsible for how you feel other than yourself. This is something that's in your control. Avoid getting overwhelmed and do not take this frustration out on your baby or even your partner.

If your baby is crying, it does not mean they are mad at you or upset with something you did. They certainly are not expressing their displeasure. Instead, this is the only means of communication for them. For instance, if your baby is crying, it's probably because the diaper has to be changed or they are sleepy. Avoid assuming the worst and ensure you never think your baby is crying because they are rejecting you.

If you believe you are unable to take your baby's crying any longer or have reached the breaking point, it is important to take a step back and take a break from whatever you are doing. Slowly distance yourself from the situation after placing the baby in the crib or handing them over to someone else in the household. Take a couple of minutes for yourself to calm down. After you feel calmer and relaxed, then go back to your baby. The simplest way to calm yourself is by taking a deep and slow breath. Count until 10 and continue to take slow breaths. Talk to a friend or a loved one for much-needed emotional support. You can also listen to calming and relaxing music. Engaging in basic household chores or responsibilities such as doing the laundry, dishes, or even cleaning a room can be relaxing. Avoid thinking about the baby or the day that lies ahead. Instead, shift all your focus to the present moment; to a specific task and give it 100%.

Sleeping

One thing that almost all new parents cannot get enough of is sleep. Depending on the baby's age, and stage of development, their sleep requirements and needs differ. That said, usually, during the first six months, babies need to be awake at night to get sufficient nourishment required for their growth and development. Babies take a while to understand how they are supposed to sleep through the night. Even if you want the baby to settle by themselves, this is a process that will take a lot of time, so be prepared.

Newborns usually need around 14-17 hours of sleep every day. Some newborns might even sleep up to 19 hours daily, which is nothing to worry about. If your baby is sleeping for prolonged periods, that is more than 4 hours at a stretch, ensure you wake them up for their regular feeding. Babies don't know when they are supposed to eat, so this is your responsibility. If your baby sleeps for longer than 3-4 hours, gently wake them and feed them. In fact, the newborn should be fed once every 3-4 hours to ensure they gain healthy weight.

Another important aspect of creating and maintaining your baby's sleeping pattern is to decide where the baby sleeps. Some believe babies should sleep in a bassinet while others believe keeping them in the crib is a better idea. Regardless of what you do, it's never a wise decision to leave the baby completely unattended. You should not allow the baby to sleep alone in swings, rockers, car seats, or any other device that is not a crib. A crib is the only place where a baby can be left alone. That said, ensure there are no toys, pillows, and blankets, and other things around that can become a potential choking hazard for the baby.

It might be quite tempting to snuggle with your little one at night. That said, avoid giving in to this temptation. Baby should never sleep on the bed or even share the bed with you. The chances of accidentally rolling over the baby are high and this cannot be ignored. According to the American Academy of Pediatrics, newborn babies should sleep in a crib or a bassinet in the parents' room. This ensures night feedings become easy and regular, and that the baby is close to the parents.

When it comes to taking care of your baby, establish certain rules for their sleep. This means your baby will get the required rest regardless of where they are. The most important rule is your baby should lie on their back while sleeping and should never be on their tummy or sides. They should only be put to sleep on a firm surface. An extra soft pillow or cushion might seem comfortable, but it increases the risk of the baby choking if they accidentally roll over. It could also promote poor posture.

Just as important as the place you put them to sleep is dressing your baby for a good night's rest. Ensure the room temperature is comfortable and the baby is not bundled up with layers of clothes. If the baby is wearing any restrictive clothes, it increases their body temperature and results in overheating. A common mistake most parents make is they believe keeping the baby awake for longer during the day means they will sleep better at night. This will only make the baby cranky. Remember, newborns will need a couple of months to learn to regularize their sleeping rhythm. In the meanwhile, they still need more than twelve hours of sleep daily. To fulfill this quota, they will take frequent naps during the day. Do not force your baby to stay awake because you believe they will sleep at night. If the baby is extremely tired or overworked, it will harm and deregulate their ability to sleep at night.

If you want your baby to sleep properly at night, creating a bedtime routine is important. Babies thrive when they have routines. Routines not only create a sense of familiarity and comfort but tell the baby what exactly they're supposed to do. A proper sleep routine is important because it gives your baby a signal or cue that it's time for them to relax and go to sleep. Routine also provides consistency which is exactly what babies need to develop healthily. An important part of creating a routine is to help them understand the difference between night and daytime. Ensure the room is always dark or dimly lit during the night. Also, it needs to be quiet. Just like adults, babies can not sleep in a noisy environment. If you need to attend to your baby's needs or even feed at night, ensure you only opt for dim lights and do not use harsh lighting. If you wake the baby up at night, regularizing their night and day or sleep rhythm becomes incredibly difficult. At night, your baby should be fed in the bedroom itself and avoid taking them elsewhere. Playtime should be restricted to the day. Even if you want to play with your baby at night, avoid doing this. Stimulating your baby at night will hamper their ability to sleep. So, nighttime should only be for creating a soothing, restful, and quiet environment.

The sleep environment plays an important role in your baby's sleeping schedule as well as their ability to sleep at night. Until your baby is at least a year old, never leave any pillows, blankets, or toys in the crib. Apart from this, ensure the room is calm, dark, and noise-free. The temperature in the room should also be comfortable and not too hot or cold.

To create a good and sustainable sleeping routine, ensure your baby goes to bed and wakes up at the same time every day. Regardless of whether it's a weekday or weekend, your baby should stick to the schedule. It's not just you, everyone in the household should follow the schedule strictly to create a proper routine.

Usually, babies want to fall asleep during feeding or after feeding. Avoid doing this. Remember, the baby should burp before they can be put to sleep. Similarly, they need to stay awake for at least 10-15 minutes after feeding to avoid spitting up or vomiting. So, avoid feeding your baby to sleep.

When you need to put your baby to sleep, don't place them in the crib when they are wide awake and active. Instead, shift them to the crib when they are half sleepy or drowsy. This gives them a while longer to get accustomed to the environment of the crib and makes it easier to fall asleep. Once they are in a comfortable environment and feel secure, their ability to sleep also improves.

Crying and fussing are quite common and expected behaviors for babies. That said, if your baby is incessantly crying and fussing regardless of all that you do, it can be a sign of an underlying health problem or condition. This is one of the reasons why you need to be extra cautious and alert during your baby's first year. You will learn more about potential health concerns and common medical problems you must pay attention to during your baby's first year later in this book.

Chapter 7: Medical Matters

First Doctor's Visit

While you may not be entirely ready for the unpredictability of feeding, crying and all-nighters, you should be ready for your baby's first doctor appointment. You must know when to schedule the appointment, the questions you should ask, and what to expect during these check-ups.

When Should Your Newborn Visit the Doctor?

The family medicine doctor or pediatrician will visit your baby a few days after the birth. During this check-up the doctor will perform the following:

● Check your baby's reflexes
● Measure the head circumference, weight, and length of your baby
● Check your baby's hearing and vision

The doctor will also tell you what to expect in the next few months and discuss your home environment with you. Technically, your baby's first appointment is going to be between three and five days after birth. If your baby has feeding issues, weight issues, or jaundice, the doctor may want to see them more often during the first few days.

Why Is The Appointment This Early?

Your baby's overall health is dependent on the first few days from birth since they are new to the world. They are still learning to sleep, feed, and adjust to a new environment. This experience is new and different for you, too. A doctor asks you to come often since they want to support you. It is for this reason they choose to see you within the first few days itself.

How Often Should You Go for Check-Ups?

Your baby's first two years are going to be packed with a lot of milestones – from the first steps to their first words. Babies will develop a lot of skills in a matter of minutes, and you will fall in love with your baby and yourself every step of the way. You need to prepare them for the future. The first 24 months of your baby's life are the most important since these create the foundation for their life. You must shape your baby's future health, wellbeing, and happiness.

Since your baby is dependent on you for everything, you are a vital part of their physical and emotional wellness. They depend on you for nourishment and expect you to protect and encourage as well. But don't worry, your baby's doctor is going to be with you every step of the way.

Importance of the Visits

Visiting your pediatrician or doctor regularly is the only way for you to determine if your baby is developing, growing, and feeding as they should. Your doctor will also tell you when to give your baby a shot to protect them from life-threatening diseases. Doctor visits are the best place to get the answers to all questions about your baby. Still, the answers to most questions or worries you have will be covered in this chapter; of course, if you have any others, don't hesitate to check with your baby's pediatrician.

When Should I Visit the Doctor?

The first visit and immunization for your baby will happen at the hospital itself. The next visits are scheduled with the doctor for 24 months:

- A few days after your baby is discharged from the hospital
- One month
- Two months
- Four months
- Six months
- Nine months
- Twelve months
- Fifteen months
- Eighteen months
- Twenty-four months

The American Academy of Pediatrics (AAP) recommends parents follow this schedule, but the doctor may alter it depending on what they believe is best for your baby. This might sound like too many visits to the pediatrician for your baby but you will inevitably have to deal with the usual upset tummy and runny nose. So, be prepared for a couple of doctor's visits at least.

The visits to the doctor are worth it. You will not only get a report about your baby reassuring you about their health but give the doctor a chance to spot issues and treat them too. Many new parents might not like the idea of their babies crying when getting a shot, but your baby needs to get all shots, so they are safe. Ensure you stay on top of this.

What to Expect During These Visits?

As the first-year progresses, you may find yourself looking forward to visiting the doctor often. These visits tell you how well your baby has developed and grown. They also will reassure and guide you in case of any concerns. Every doctor visit will be different, but your doctor will do all or some of the following each time:

- Answer any questions you have about your baby. Ensure you note down the questions if you are worried about forgetting them.
- Check with you about how you and your baby are doing, your baby's development, feeding, and sleep cycle.
- Measure your baby's head circumference, length, and weight. The doctor also plots this information on the growth chart to check your baby's progress.

Perform a physical exam to check the following:

- Breathing and heartbeat using a stethoscope
- Legs, back, arms, spine, and hips to ensure they move as expected and are growing normally
- Press the belly gently to check if there is anything different
- Use an otoscope to check the nose and ears
- Check the throat, mouth, and eyes
- Press the lymph glands in the underarms and neck to see if there are any issues
- Check the soft spots (fontanelles) on your baby's head
- Check your baby for undescended testicles or hernias. The doctor may also check if there is a steady and strong femoral pulse in your baby's groin
- Reflexes depending on your baby's age
- Check the skin for any birthmarks

If your baby should take any vaccinations, the nurse or doctor will administer it. Most doctors leave this for the end to ensure your baby is relaxed and happy before he gives the shot. During the examination, you can speak to your doctor comfortably and get all your questions answered. So, when your baby is administered the shot, you have the full attention to calm them down.

Making the Most of the Visits

Are you wondering how you can manage your baby and still remember the questions you wanted to ask the doctor? You must also remember all the answers he gives you. Therefore, be prepared.

Timing Is Right

You cannot expect all appointments to be scheduled at opportune times. You cannot always avoid fussy times, nap times, and mealtimes; this is especially difficult if your baby does not have a routine. If your pediatrician is flexible, you can try to schedule your visit when your baby is well-fed and well-rested. You can also schedule your visit when your baby is usually on their best behavior. It is also important to schedule the visit when the doctor's office is not going to be packed. The office is going to be busy before work and after school, so confirm with the doctor before you schedule the visit. It is generally best to schedule the appointment immediately when the office opens or after lunch.

Create A Checklist

You have to carry a lot of things when you visit the doctor, including a change of clothes, diapers, insurance card, and burp cloth. Place things in the bag the night before you have the visit, so it is easier for you to get out on time. The following are what you must carry:

- Change of clothes
- Wipes and diapers
- Insurance information
- Burp cloths
- Your baby's favorite object, toy, or blanket
- A blanket to place over the doctor's table
- A full bottle, if your baby is okay with bottle-feeding
- A pacifier or teething ring
- A list of all your baby's abilities and skills, including information about dirty diapers, feeding times, and sleep record
- If you are visiting a new doctor, list your baby's medical history
- A list of concerns and questions you want to ask your doctor
- Snacks and food if you are feeding your baby solids, and for yourself

List All Your Questions

Maintain a list of all questions (urgent and non-urgent) and concerns on a notepad or your phone, so you have them ready for your doctor's visit. You may be worried about when your baby will sleep, how much weight they should be gaining, if you are burping them right, and so on. The list is never-ending. You must speak to your doctor about these concerns when you visit them. They will reassure you and tell you all you need to know. If your baby has trouble with breastfeeding, you may need to visit a lactation consultant, as well.

Know Your Baby

You know your baby better than anybody else, so you should tell the doctor everything they need to know about your baby. They are going to ask you about your baby's milestones, so tell them everything. Brag about it. You can use an app to track your baby's feeding time, sleep duration, dirty and wet diapers to make this information more readily available. Your doctor will want and appreciate all this information.

Dress Your Baby Well

When you take your baby to the doctor, they will be undressed. So, think of an outfit you can easily remove and put back on. It is cute to dress your baby in a cute onesie, but it is going to be a task if you should remove them from the onesie quickly. It becomes difficult if they are squirmy and irritable. The same goes for any tight clothes. As mentioned earlier, carry a backup outfit.

Vaccinations

Your baby is born with certain antibodies since some from the mother move to the baby while still in the womb. If your baby is being breastfed, the antibodies from the mother are still being passed to the baby. Unfortunately, the protection in both cases is only temporary and not strong enough for life. The only way to build your baby's immunity completely is through immunization. In some cases, your baby is administered weakened or killed germs causing a specific disease (vaccination). Other times your baby is administered a tiny piece, such as a piece of the germ's genetic material or protein.

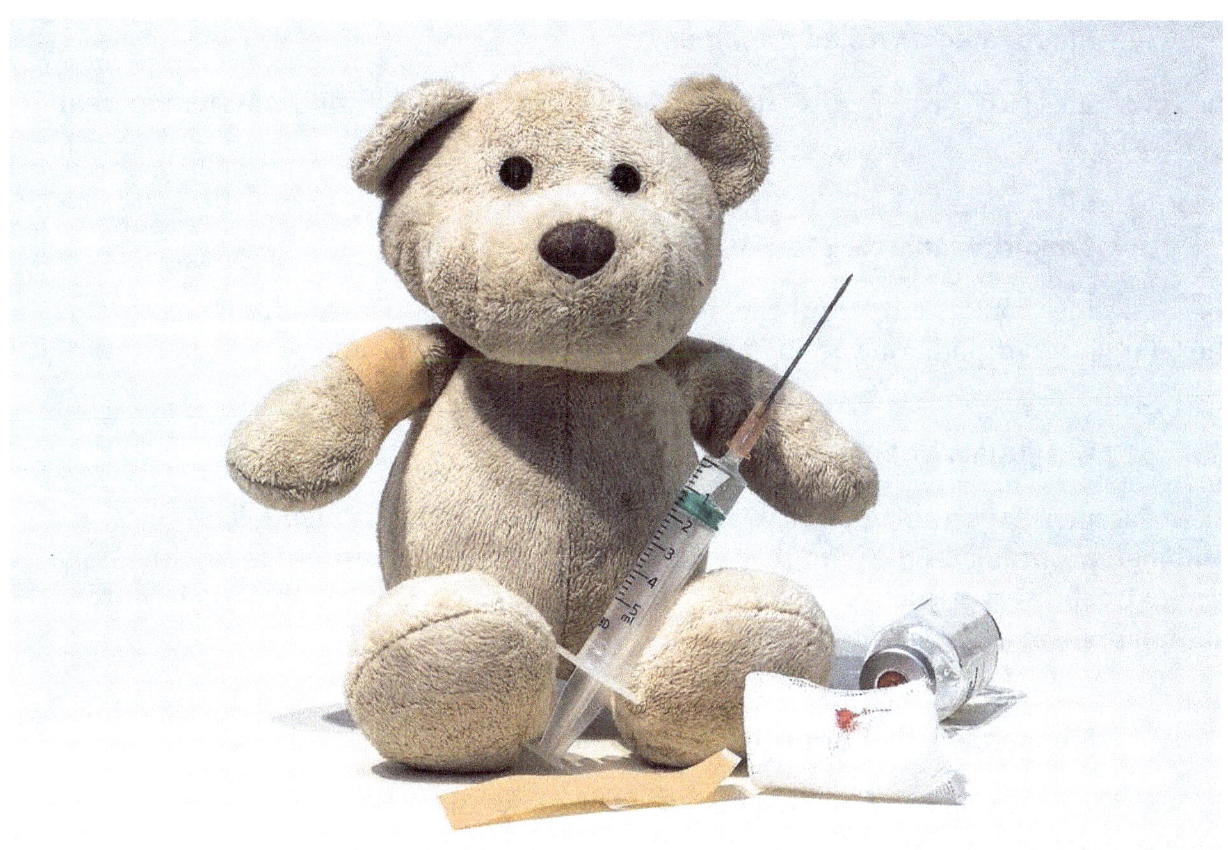

These germs can either be bacteria or viruses. Through vaccinations, your baby's immune system is activated, and it reacts to the administered germs the way it would react to the real infection. It will kill the germ and fend off the infection. This is the only way for the immune system to remember this germ. This is the only way your baby can remain healthy if the germ enters their body later.

Different Types Of Vaccines

AAP recommends babies get a combination of different vaccines, listed below, instead of one type of vaccine. The different types include:

Weakened or Attenuated Vaccines

These vaccines have weakened germs and are used to help your baby's body fight rubella, measles, and mumps. Your baby may also be given a shot of the chickenpox vaccine if you are willing.

Inactivated or Killed Vaccines

These vaccines have dead germs and are used to stimulate the immune system to treat polio or flu.

Toxoid Vaccines

These vaccines contain a harmful chemical the germ created to introduce the body to it. The tetanus and diphtheria vaccines are examples of toxoid vaccines.

Conjugate Vaccines

These vaccines have a small piece of the germ along with other proteins. This combination stimulates the immune system to trigger a strong response. Vaccines are used to treat diseases, such as meningitis, hepatitis B, whooping cough and HPV are examples of conjugate vaccines.

Messenger RNA or mRNA Vaccines

These vaccines have a piece of the germ's genetic material (or RNA). Not many such vaccines exist, but some COVID vaccines are mRNA vaccines.
Doctors give babies a combination of vaccines, so the little one is not stabbed too many times. This is a safe way to care for the baby. Since your baby is exposed to numerous germs when they are born, they must be vaccinated, to handle any germs in the future.

Vaccinations Your Baby Needs

AAP recommends the following vaccinations to be administered to your baby. Bear in mind that some of these vaccinations may vary depending on new developments. Your doctor will tell you about the vaccinations your baby must take and when to schedule each.

- Measles, mumps, and rubella vaccine (MMR)
- Chickenpox (varicella) vaccine
- Hepatitis A vaccine (HepA)
- Rotavirus vaccine (RV)
- Diphtheria, tetanus, and pertussis vaccine (DTaP)
- Pneumococcal vaccines (PCV13, PPSV23)
- Hepatitis B vaccine (HepB)
- Human papillomavirus (HPV) vaccine

- Influenza vaccine
- Meningococcal vaccines (MenACWY, MenB)
- Haemophilus influenzae type b (Hib) vaccine
- Polio vaccine (IPV)
- COVID-19 vaccine

Concerns

If you are worried about vaccinating your baby, know you are not alone. Some parents have worries or questions about strong reactions to the vaccine. Some are worried their babies may get the infection. It is important to remember the components of any vaccine are killed or weakened. As discussed above, in some cases only a part of the germ is taken, so the chances of illness are slim. Yes, your baby may have mild reactions, such as a fever or soreness where the shot was given, but the chances of them having a serious reaction is rare. The risks of the illness are more when compared to that of a vaccination. It is important to vaccinate your baby, so they are protected against contagious diseases.

Vaccination Schedule

According to the CDC, the following schedule must be followed. There may be variations depending on your doctor's examinations of your baby.

- At birth: First dose of HepB vaccine
- 1 – 2 months: Second dose of HepB vaccine
- 2 and 4 months: DTaP, Hib, IPV, PCV, and RV
- 6 months: Third dose of above vaccines, except for IPB. The doctor may also recommend the flu shot
- Between 6 and 18 months: IPV and HepB
- Between 12 and 15 months: Hib, MMR, PCV, and Varicella
- Between 12 and 23 months: HepA
- Between 15 and 18 months: DTaP
- Between 4 and 6 years: Varicella, DTaP, IPV, and MMR
- Between 11 and 12 years: Tdap, HPV, COVID-19, and MenACWY
- Between 16 and 18 years: MenB

Common Illnesses

Since your baby is being introduced to a new environment, they are bound to pick up some germs and infections. Do not let this worry you, because all or most of these can be treated easily. Some of the illnesses include:

- Colic
- Cold and Flu
- Ear Infections
- Constipation
- Diarrhea
- Digestive problems
- Skin rashes and infections
- Allergies

You need to identify the symptoms to treat the issues early. The doctor may also identify some issues based on the notes you make about your baby. Therefore, ensure you have the most accurate and correct information you can give your doctor.

Keeping Your Baby Healthy

If you want your baby to stay healthy, you must ensure they are active and happy. Keep them away from anything dangerous, such as an electric socket, drawers, windows, and more. In short, baby-proof your house. Use the following tips to ensure your baby is healthy and happy.

- An active baby is a happy baby. Let them lie down on the floor and crawl. This is a great way to strengthen their body. It also gives them a chance to explore the environment they are in.
- Avoid leaving your baby in strollers, swings, exercise saucers, and bouncer seats.
- It is best to avoid screens around your baby. Instead, read and play hands-on with them. AAP suggests that parents avoid screen media around children under 18 months. You can use these media if it is inevitable. Such as video calling family.
- Wash your hands before you pick up your baby, and ensure others do so too.
- Your baby is susceptible to illnesses. Therefore, leave your footwear outside your house, so you do not carry any germs in. Wash up and change your outside clothing before you handle your baby.
- When your baby's teeth appear, brush them.

Keeping Your Baby Safe

Your baby is already having a tough time adjusting to things around them. So, you have to keep them safe. Use the following tips to ensure your baby is in your presence or proper care.

Prevent Strangulation and Suffocation

- If your baby sleeps in a crib, ensure the slats are not too far apart. Anything less than 2 3/8th of an inch is good. You must also use sheets that cover the mattress snugly.
- The minute your baby can pull themself up using the crib's side as support, remove it. You should also get rid of mobiles.
- Do not leave any bags, especially plastic around your child.
- Tie up any cords to ensure your baby does not touch them.
- Remove any drawstrings or cords from your baby's clothing. It is best to avoid buying clothes with either of those.
- Rearrange your furniture, so your baby does not have access to any cords.

Prevent Choking and Ingestion of Substances

Yes, your baby is going to pick up everything in their sight and more often than not put it into their mouth. This is inevitable. Having said that, you can protect them by minimizing access to these substances.

- Keep all medicines, harmful substances, and cleaners in a cabinet. Lock the storage place if it is within your child's reach.
- No plants around your child. They might tear the leaves and even try to eat the soil.
- Do not give your baby hard candies, grapes, popcorn, raisins, carrots, or nuts since they can easily choke on them.

Prevent Burns

Do not cook while you hold your baby since this is the most dangerous thing to do. If your baby is crawling around you while you cook, turn the pot handles away from you, so you do not bump into them causing food or hot water to spill on your baby. Move cords away from your baby, especially if they are on a high chair in your kitchen.

Prevent Falls

Your baby is going to fall. This is something you should expect. You can, however, protect them from having bad falls. For instance, if you have a staircase at home, keep it gated, so they don't trip and fall down the stairs. Even if you keep your baby strapped to a changing table, hold them. They are going to squirm, and you cannot only rely on the strap. It is also important to never leave them alone in a bed or sofa.

First Aid Tips

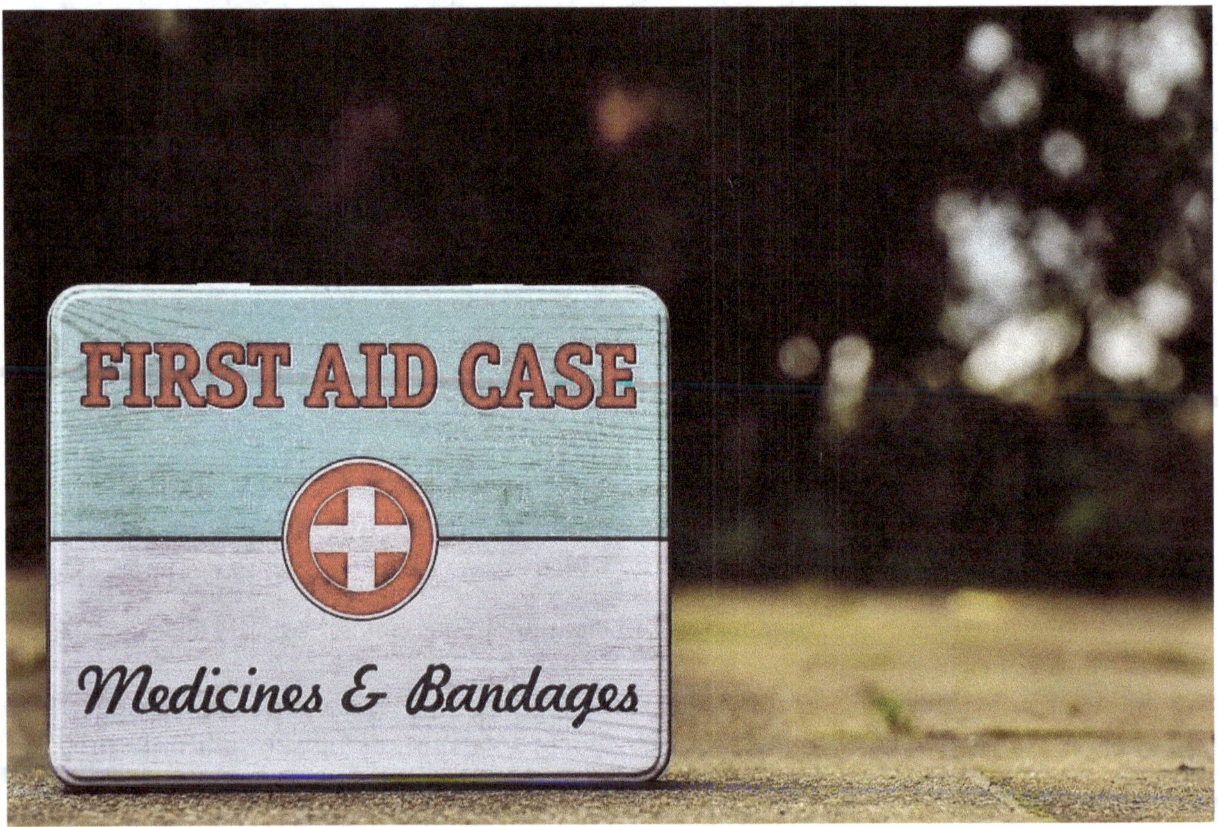

You must know some first aid tips when you have a baby at home. If they have a small wound, learn to clean and wrap it quickly to prevent infection. You should also know when to call someone for help. In this section, we will cover some tips you can use in any crisis. The tips mentioned in this section are only to protect your baby from further harm.

Kit Essentials

You must have a few supplies handy in your first aid kit for your baby. If you want to make things easier, keep a separate kit only for your baby. Ensure your parents, nanny or friends know where to find this kit if you are not around. The following are some essentials to include in your baby's kit:

● Antibiotic cream (safe for ages 2+)
● Baby brush or comb
● Baby gas drops (AAP-approved Simethicone)
● Baby nail clippers
● Baby thermometer
● Blunt scissors
● Bulb syringe/ nasal aspirator
● Cotton balls (Don't use swabs to clean baby's nose or ears.)
● Infant Acetaminophen (brand name Tylenol, safe after 12 weeks)
● Infant toothbrush
● Medicine dropper
● Petroleum jelly and sterile gauze (for circumcision care)
● Saline nasal drops (AAP-approved in place of cough and cold medicine)

If your baby or young child is hurt, it is important to assess the situation and find what caused them harm. You can ensure their surroundings are safe before you administer first aid. Assess how hurt they are. Firstly see if their reflexes are working fine by flicking their foot. Then listen to their breathing and check their pulse. Keep the following points in mind:

● If your baby is having trouble breathing, tilt their head back a little to open the airway.
● If your baby is not breathing, call 911 immediately. If you know how to perform CPR, do it until your baby breathes or the EMTs have reached your house.
● If your baby is responsive and breathing, check them fully before you call 911.

Additional Tips

In case your child has:

● A runny nose: Use suction to remove the mucus from their nose.
● Scrapes and cuts: Clean the wound before you cover it with gauze or a band-aid.
● Insect bites: Clean the wound and see if you can spot the insect. Most insect wounds give your baby a fever, so do not worry if they have a slight temperature. If you want to be thorough, go to the doctor at once.

- Head bumps: Your baby is going to bump their head a lot. Most bumps heal quickly, but if you see a bump persisting for longer than a day, visit the doctor since it can mean your baby has a concussion.
- Choking, strangulation, or suffocation: Identify why your baby feels this way. Open the airway by tilting their head. If they are still having trouble breathing, call 911.
- Consuming dangerous food: Since your baby is inquisitive, they are going to try to eat everything within their reach. This is not something you can stop. If you see them putting something dangerous in their mouth, stop them. Put your fingers in their mouth and see if you can pull the substance out. If you cannot, go to the doctor.
- Burns and scalds: If your baby touches something hot, pour cold water on the part. Apply easy and natural burn medicine, like aloe.

You are going to be worried when you hear your baby cry. Do not let this worry cloud your judgment. Use the tips in the book to make a quick assessment before you call the doctor. If your baby was bitten by a poisonous insect or snake, bring them to the emergency unit. Keep the following information handy:

- If you need to call 911, keep your home phone number and address near you
- Your own cell number
- List of medicines your child is taking
- Any allergies your child has
- The pediatrician's number
- The Poison Helpline: 800-222-1222

When To Call 911

Do not call 911 every time your child hurts themself. Call the emergency number if they are not breathing, turning blue, unconscious, or lethargic. If your baby is unresponsive, irritable, refuses to eat, has trouble breathing, has a broken bone, is dehydrated, or has a similar symptom, immediately bring them to the ER. If you are unsure of what the situation is, speak to your personal doctor before you call 911.

When To Call Your Doctor

Call your doctor in any of the following situations:

- Tear ducts are blocked
- Fever is consistently above 100.4F or 38C and persists for longer than 24 hours
- Sick symptoms even after the body temperature is normal
- Difficulty breathing
- Dehydration, vomiting, or diarrhea

● Has yellow skin or eyes
● Has a terrible cold for longer than 2 days

Before you call your doctor, ensure you have a pen and paper near you to write down any instructions. You should also have the following information handy:

● Immunization records
● The names and doses of any medications
● Any medical problems your baby may have

Children grow and develop at their own pace, but there is a guideline we will discuss in the next chapter. You can use these to follow your child's growth. If your child does not follow this pattern or sequence, voice out your concerns to your doctor. They can reassure you or let you know if anything is amiss.

Chapter 8: Your Baby's Development

In this chapter, we will cover the developmental milestones for your baby during the first year. We will also look at some activities we can do to maximize their development. Your baby is going to change a lot in the first year of their life. Most babies without certain conditions develop and grow in the following areas:

- Physical: Your baby is going to grow taller and chubbier depending on their food intake and activity level. While it is okay to have a chubby baby, ensure their weight is within the approved limits.
- Cognitive: They are going to respond to your tone and words, and begin to recognize people around them. They will let you know through their actions who they are most comfortable to be around.
- Social and emotional: Your child is either going to enjoy being around people or not. So, watch them and learn from their actions. If they tell you who they are comfortable around, allow only those people to hold them. Despite what people say, babies do not like being paraded around. Work to understand them and do what they are most comfortable with.
- Language: Most babies start making sounds, and it almost feels like they are conversing with you every time you say something to them. They may not form the right words yet, but they are trying.
- Sensory and motor: Your baby is going to flip in a few months and start crawling soon. This is a major milestone since it means your baby is going to start walking and running in a short while.

Milestones

Since your baby is going to develop quite a bit during the first year, you must track some important milestones. Your doctor is going to ask you about these during your visits.

Between One and Three Months

The following are some general milestones babies are expected to meet. Do not fret if your baby does not meet these milestones at the exact pace as expected. Give them time.

- Smiling
- Lifting their head and chest when they are lying on their tummy
- Tracking objects and movements
- Moving their hands to their mouth
- Opening and closing their palms
- Swiping and reaching for hair, glasses, and other objects
- Grabbing and holding objects in their hand

If you want to further encourage your baby to reach these milestones, you can perform some activities with them during this growing period.

● Use activities involving sensory play.
● Walk around with your baby, so they know what the world looks like.
● Let your baby rest on the floor on their tummy.
● Keep talking to them and naming things around them.
● Recite and sing rhymes.

Between Four and Six Months

The following are some milestones your baby may reach during this period:

● Rolling over or back depending on how you have them sleep
● Laughing
● Babbling
● Grabbing objects
● Crushing or manipulating objects
● Trying to sit up with support
● Controlling their head movements
● Sleeping through the night (Thank God!)

To ensure your baby meets these milestones, perform one or more of the following activities:

● Your baby cannot say words, so you can teach them sign language. Even if they don't fully understand, it is worth giving it a try. Simple gestures can refer to actions or objects.
● Let them play with play dough.
● Carry them and dance around the house like nobody's watching.

Between Seven and Nine Months

Here are some of the milestones your baby will reach during this period.

● Sitting alone
● Crawling and waving their arms
● Waving their arms to say bye
● Whenever they hear a voice or a sound, they turn in that direction
● Start imitating sounds
● Chewing on different objects
● Dropping objects and learning to pick up tiny objects
● Start identifying their reflection in the mirror
● Responding and reacting to their names
● Learning to distinguish different emotions according to tone or voice

To help your baby reach all these milestones, a little extra effort from your side will not hurt. Here are some activities you can engage with your little ones to help them achieve their developmental milestones.

● Playing with made-at-home instruments or musical toys will be quite exciting for your baby during this period. Any activity that incorporates music, sounds, and lets them practice their motor movements is incredibly helpful.
● You can start teaching them to play hide and seek. You don't have to run around the house. Instead, simply hide a little away from your baby and ask them to find you.
● Start imitating your baby's actions to encourage further movement.
● Lay some comfortable cushions on the floor, ask your baby to climb on them and jump off them. Don't let your baby do this activity without adult supervision.

Between Ten and Twelve Months

Here are some milestones your baby might reach before they are 12 months old.

● Become incredibly inquisitive and start popping anything that comes within their reach into the mouth.
● Start self-feeding.
● Standing briefly without any additional support.
● Taking their first steps with some support.

This is an incredibly exciting time because babies will begin taking their first steps. While most babies usually do this just over the 9-month mark, some take a bit longer; it may not be until they are 13 months old. During these months they will learn by holding onto furniture or specifically designed stepping toys and holders for support. They typically cannot begin cruising during this stage.
It is also during the 9-12 month period that babies will begin uttering their first words. So exciting!
To ensure that your baby meets all their developmental milestones before they are 12 months old, don't forget to get them engaged in interesting activities.

● Babies are quick learners and are naturally inquisitive. Make the most of these traits by reading books. Choosing any book that has different activities, textures, colorful images, and flaps will come in handy. Reading also helps them in learning to imitate sounds and make words.
● Ensure that you constantly talk to your baby. Regular conversations help keep your baby engaged.
● This is the time to start establishing limits about what is and is not acceptable in terms of your baby's behavior.
● Start teaching your baby to learn about emotions. Whenever you notice your baby is feeling cranky, ensure that you mention the specific emotion and talk to them calmly.

● To engage and promote better motor development and coordination use water play. Always supervise them closely with or around water.

Don't Get Worried

We are all different and so are our babies. Babies grow and develop at different paces according to a variety of factors. The timing window within which a baby is expected to reach a developmental milestone is fairly wide. There are no hard and fast rules about what your baby should be doing. Instead, they are just general expectations. Some babies develop quicker when compared to others. This is nothing to worry about. For instance, some babies start walking a little after reaching the 1-year mark while others don't take their first step until they are 18 months old. Similarly, some might utter their first word when they are 8 months old while others might need a few more months. This is one of the reasons why you should never get stressed or worried about your baby's development.

Do not make the mistake of selecting and laying down the developmental milestones they need to hit. Instead, let your baby develop at its own pace. This means you need to let them take the lead.

That said, here are some simple activities and steps to ensure and promote your baby's healthy development.

A simple way to promote your baby's ability to communicate is by constantly talking to them. Have frequent conversations with them. Whenever your baby makes a sound, respond to it and add a couple of words coupled with the sound they made. Read stories to your baby. Sing and play music. Whenever they make any sounds, ensure you give them a little attention. Apart from this, praising your baby, talking to them in an excited tone, and having animated and expressive conversations helps.

You need to make your baby feel safe and secure. The simplest way to do this is through physical contact. The power of physical comfort cannot be underestimated. From hugs to cuddles and kisses, there are a lot of ways to express your love. Ensure you do all of them to make your baby feel loved, safe, and comfortable. When all these three needs are consistently taken care of, your baby's development will improve.

Whenever your baby looks alert or relaxed, ensure that you play with them. Do not play with your baby by waking them up from sleep. Make sure no one else does this as well. Whenever they look active, make the most of it. If your baby starts moving to areas that they shouldn't or touch things they shouldn't come up with a way to distract and gently redirect their attention.

While conversing with your baby, ensure that you do not order them around. Instead, gently talk to them. This is especially true if your baby is close to reaching the 12-month mark. By now, babies can make sounds, and maybe even crawl or walk. Instead of shouting commands, talk to them excitedly.

Ensure they have plenty of room to move. Do not confine them to small spaces. Whenever possible, take them to outdoor parks. Whenever you go out, ensure they are safe and properly dressed. Additionally, you will need to find some challenging activities for your baby. Whenever you are playing with interactive toys or reading interactive storybooks, ensure your baby is thoroughly engaged in the activity and is not distracted. Even though babies develop at different rates, chances are you will inevitably be worried about their development. The first thing you must do is consult your baby's pediatrician. They should be your primary authority when it comes to your baby's well-being and development. If you have any worries or concerns, get in touch with your baby's healthcare provider. As stated previously before meeting the doctor, ensure that you have a record or notes about any concerns or worrying developments you have noticed. Usually, your baby's development should be screened using standardized and validated tools once they are 9, 18, and 30-months-old for overall general development. On the other hand, they must be screened once they are 18 and 24 months old for signs of autism.

Continue to consult with your pediatrician throughout your baby's development. If needed, you might be referred to a specialist for thorough evaluation and analysis. Some common specialists you might have to consult if your baby is facing developmental delays include developmental pediatricians, child psychiatrists or psychologists, and child neurologists.

Taking care of a baby is a full-time responsibility. There are no breaks. This is especially true during the first year of the baby's life. Some parents are hyper-focused on everything their baby says and does. They spend all their waking moments catering only to the baby's needs that they can forget about themselves. Dear new dad, do not do this. You and your partner are humans too. Never become so engrossed with your baby that you forget about concentrating on yourself. Unless you take care of yourselves, you cannot do the best for your baby.

Chapter 9: Don't Forget Yourselves

As soon as a baby arrives, the relationship shared with your partner will change inevitably. That said, you can also make the relationship stronger with a little extra and conscious effort. When a baby takes priority over everything else, it's easy to forget about ourselves. It will sooner or later adversely affect the relationship. When your baby takes the center stage, it will feel as if your entire life is structured around their schedule. Whether it is their feeding, sleeping, or changing schedules, you will reschedule your days to accommodate their needs and the routine you set.

During the first couple of weeks of bringing a baby home, parents seldom get any rest. This is because babies need to be fed and changed constantly, and you also need to deal with their crying. A combination of all these factors can leave new parents feeling annoyed, irritated, and exhausted. This increases the chances of having misunderstandings and unnecessary arguments. It also means feelings are hurt. So, it is important to always remember you and your partner are on the same team. You are a team catering to your baby's needs. Don't forget this.

Common Couple Issues After Baby

To improve the relationship with your partner, it's important to understand the most common problems or issues couples fight over once a baby arrives.

Dealing With Chores and Duties

Perhaps the most common issue is the sharing of chores and duties. There will be plenty of things to be done. If you or your partner starts keeping a track of the number of chores and duties you are each responsible for, it can lead to unnecessary bickering that can manifest as resentment. A simple option is to equally divide the chores and make a list of duties or tasks. Post a list of the chores on the fridge and start switching responsibilities every other week. This means you are both taking care of all the same things the other has done.

Another effective option to avoid fighting over chores and duties is to divide the tasks according to your strengths and preferences. For instance, if you are taking over the duty of cleaning up after dinner and taking out the trash, perhaps your spouse can take care of loading the utensils into the dishwasher.

Different Parenting Styles

We are all different and therefore, we have different thoughts, opinions, and ideas. This means the parenting styles you and your partner opt for will be different. It is wonderful if you are both on the same page; but even if you are not, it is not a reason to engage in unhelpful power struggles. Before writing off someone else's parenting style, try to learn about it and see how it works. For instance, if you believe in establishing strict rules the child should follow but your partner is more of a permissive parent, it will not work. Instead, it will raise a confused child. To avoid this, spend some time, and discuss the pros and cons of each other's parenting styles. Create a style that works well for you both.

Excess Family Involvement

Everyone has different opinions about how children are to be raised or what parents are supposed to do. Unfortunately, unsolicited advice creates more problems than solutions. For instance, grandparents might want to spend too much time with the baby. If so, it's important to establish boundaries. For now, you need to concentrate on tending to your family — your spouse, baby, and you. Because it is your baby, you have a right to say no regardless of how generous other family members have been with gifts or time for your little one. Even if they are babysitting, it's important to draw some boundaries. A simple yet effective means to establish and maintain boundaries is creating a weekly schedule that allocates specific time the grandparents can spend with your baby.

Money Matters

One topic that can uproot even the strongest of relationships is finances. You and your partner must be on the same page about finances. This is one topic where you both need to be brutally honest with each other. Take a step back and frankly discuss your finances. Make a list of things that matter, the expenses you are incurring, and the projected growth of expenses. Apart from this, consider your savings and earnings options. If you notice any areas where spending should be curbed, talk to your partner about it. The simplest way to avoid all this is by ensuring every decision is made collectively. Stop deciding for your partner and vice versa. If there are any areas where you believe you don't agree or see eye to eye, discuss it calmly and try to find the middle ground.

Getting Alone Time

Getting some time to recover, rest, and relax is important. With a baby at home, it might feel like you will never get any alone time. Well, alone time is an important part of your self-care routine. Self-care is about taking small chunks of time daily and keeping it to yourself so you don't feel trapped as a new parent. Yes, it is quite possible to feel suffocated due to this responsibility. This is why balance is needed. When you start taking care of yourself, it becomes easier to maintain your physical and mental well-being. When you are functioning optimally, both physically and mentally, it becomes easier to take care of your baby. You can become the parent your baby needs.

To do this, you will need to get some time alone. So do not deny yourself or your partner some time to rest and relax. You are both individuals with different preferences and interests. There is no reason why you shouldn't hold onto your interests. It's about finding a little balance. Setting aside 20-30 minutes daily for self-care or doing things that you enjoy is not as difficult as it may seem. This is also needed to maintain your emotional and mental well-being.

Simple and effective means to take care of yourself include consuming healthy and wholesome meals. Ensure you and your partner eat plenty of protein, iron, healthy fats, instead of unhealthy sugars and processed foods. Whenever possible, strap on the baby carrier and take your baby for a stroll. This means you can spend more time with them outdoors while your partner gets a chance to relax. It is also a simple way to exercise while taking care of the baby.

Whenever your baby falls asleep, your priority should also be to sleep. This may be the only chance you get to rest. It can be quite tempting to catch up on all the chores or responsibilities but put it on hold until later. For now, ensure you are getting sufficient rest.

Spend some time outdoors. Try your hand at meditation. And ensure you don't alienate your friends and other relations right now. We are all social beings and regardless of how much time the baby takes, it's not okay to compromise on other social aspects of your life. Apart from all this, accept each other's help. You don't have to do it all. Remember, you are a team.

Learn to say no and don't take on more than you can handle. For now, concentrate on your family until your baby is accustomed to a predictable schedule. Even if it seems like you are putting your life on hold, it is only a temporary situation. So, cut yourself some slack. Dear parents, parenting is not easy. It is okay to focus on yourselves too.

Quality Time for New Parents

You might want to spend every waking minute with your baby. That said, it's equally important to spend some alone time with your partner too. So, create a schedule where you can spend time with your partner without the baby. During this period, concentrate on each other and talk about what you're feeling. Share the highlights of your day, any problems you are facing, or even any concerns you have. Make it a point to spend time with each other at least once a week. During your weekly date night avoid talking about baby care or anything associated with the household. Instead, go back to how date nights are supposed to be. Focus on yourself and don't let this be run over with topics about the baby.

The sexual aspect of a relationship cannot be ignored. Even though sex doesn't define the relationship, it's a part of a healthy and happy relationship. Usually, it is recommended to wait for four-six weeks after birth before having sex to reduce the risk of infections. It also ensures your partner is fully healed and there is no scope for internal bleeding. You will need to discuss when you want to resume sexual activities with your partner. Apart from this, consult her healthcare provider as well to obtain the required information. You can start slow with simple things such as kissing, cuddling, and snuggling before moving on to more intimate sexual activities.

You both need to be open and honest when it comes to talking about sex. Ensure that your partner is comfortable and is not doing anything only because you want to. Don't make her feel cornered or pressured into having sex before she is ready. She might be scared of the pains she could experience. In such instances, time is all that's needed. Also, it's important to consider the means of protection you want to use. Getting pregnant during the postpartum period is quite easy. To prevent accidental pregnancy, you will need to include different methods of protection such as condoms, an IUD, pills, and any other method prescribed by a healthcare practitioner.

Before resuming activities in the boudoir, ensure that you talk to your partner about what she would like to do. When she is ready, ask her what feels comfortable to her, and the positions she likes. If her vagina is not as moist as usual, especially during breastfeeding times, using water-based lubricant helps. Apart from this, you will also need to make time for sex. Even if impromptu romps are not possible, you can schedule some time for yourself.

Tips for Getting Through Issues

Arguments and disagreements are a common part of any relationship. All that matters is how you deal with them. Ultimately, it's about strengthening your bond instead of saying things you know will cause the most damage. Here are some simple suggestions that can be used to get through any issues you face as a couple.

If you are upset with something your partner says or does, concentrate on asking them to change a specific aspect of their behavior— instead of making generalized character indictments. If you are or were wrong, said something for the sake of hurting your partner, or snapped unnecessarily, ensure you apologize immediately. Don't just say you are sorry, but ensure you apologize for the specific action you believe has hurt your partner.

Never assume how your partner is feeling, instead ask them. No one is a mind reader and therefore, it's impossible to understand how the other person is truly feeling. Whenever your partner expresses something, ensure you listen to them and convey the same by paraphrasing what they said. While resolving any disagreements, the idea is not to prove yourself right or prove your point; instead, it is about working together as a team to solve your problems.

Whenever you are facing any issue, give each other a chance to fully express your feelings. For example, you can establish a rule that you will both stick to a three-sentence limit. Once you have said your three sentences, wait for your partner to respond. This also gives you a chance to calm down and think about what you are saying

Whenever you're solving problems, concentrate only on the issue at hand. Bringing the past into the pictures doesn't help. If you have unresolved issues, ensure you talk to your partner about them. If it feels like things are getting a little too heated, it is better to take a step back. Give yourself a 20 minute out and resume the discussion once you are both calm.

Support System

There are two support networks all new parents need: a healthcare network and a personal network. The point of these support networks is to give a little extra assistance, especially when the going gets tough. You and your partner are both human, and therefore, cannot do everything on your own. You both might be each other's primary support system, but there are certain things where others need to help as well. After all, it takes a village to raise a child.

Your personal support system will consist of family members, friends, coworkers, and any other loved ones. It can also include your neighbors, social workers, community groups, religious congregations, or even other expecting families. It's always better to know you can count and depend on others in your time of need. Knowing you have a support system itself is motivating enough to keep going. When you can share your problems or worries with others and realize you are not alone, your ability to get through a situation also improves.

Your healthcare support network must include a local pharmacist, dietitian, family doctor, midwife or obstetrician for your partner, nurses, dentists, and your baby's pediatrician. It's always better to keep all these contacts on hand in case of an emergency.

Ask for Help

You don't have to do everything on your own. It is okay to ask for help; we all have our limitations. Asking for help doesn't mean you cannot do something on your own or you're not good at it. Instead, it just means you need a little extra assistance to work through the situation. Getting acclimatized to parenthood will take some time, so be open to all the help and support you receive.

Don't just wait for others to offer; feel comfortable asking for help whenever you need it. If you think you need something, ask. You don't have to hesitate or feel shy. Remember, you are not imposing or demanding. Instead, you're making a humble request. To ensure you don't feel awkward, clarify what you need, and don't be afraid to follow up. You can also keep your daily to-do list on hand while doing this.

Go back to your support system and think about different chores which can be delegated. For instance, picking up laundry, weekly grocery shopping, or monthly medical supplies are simple tasks that can be outsourced or delegated. Once you delegate, ensure that you follow through as well. You don't have to feel self-conscious about reaching out. Even if you do, you can find someone else who can request it on your behalf.

Chapter 10: Savoring Your First Year As A Family Of Three

Now, you are no longer a family of two but are a family of three. This wonderful addition will bring more joy and love to your life. That said, your baby's first year will be overwhelming, incredibly exhausting, and even stressful at times. All it takes is a little adjustment. As you start adjusting to this new role, you'll realize it is incredibly fulfilling. It truly is a magical experience. All the little moments you start sharing with your baby help strengthen your bond. The moments spent with your partner lay down the foundation for a solid family relationship. These are also the moments that will energize and invigorate you.

All you need to do is pause for a moment and savor them. Don't get so caught up doing things that you forget about living in the moment and enjoying each day.

Learning to relish the little moments and all the small details about your baby will improve your emotional wellbeing and make your life more satisfying. Even science says cherishing the good times creates stronger bonds between parents and their babies (Burkhart et al. 2015). So, what's the catch? The problem is most of us are constantly thinking about the future or worrying about the past and we forget about the present. Unless you pause and be mindfully present to appreciate the little moments, it will pass you by within the blink of an eye. Don't let these moments disappear and become more mindful. Mindfulness is the simple practice of living in the moment without entertaining thoughts about the past or future. This practice will make you a better partner and parent.

To acknowledge the little moments and relish them, you will need to declutter your life. It means you'll need to start getting rid of everything and anything that prevents you from enjoying your life to the fullest and living in the moment. For instance, if you are constantly distracted by work, you cannot fully be present while tending to your baby. Similarly, a weekend visit to the zoo is meaningless if you are on constant work-related phone calls. It's not about giving up on working. Instead, it is about learning to prioritize and drawing strong boundaries. Establish fixed times for your work and ensure you are with your family after work hours. Stop carrying your work home, at least for a couple of months. Remember, you need to help your partner as well. A baby's first year is full of milestones. From their first smile to the time they learn to roll over or start crawling, there are so many different little things. If you are not careful, you will miss them.

Ensure that you do not overschedule yourself or your baby. Yes, spending time together is important. But if you are actively trying to create big memories or are trying to do a dozen external things, your schedule will become overwhelming. Also, it can overstimulate and overwhelm your little one. Instead of all this, take a couple of minutes to reflect on the small moments you have lived through. For instance, it can be something as simple as your baby eagerly waving their arms as you come home from work, or babbling of random sounds and noises whenever they are happy. These are the moments you need to learn to rejoice. These are the memories that will stay for a lifetime. Whenever possible, make it a point to acknowledge the moment with a couple of gestures or words. For instance, if your baby is excitedly waving their arms at you, you should respond similarly. If there is something you appreciate about your partner, make a note of it. Sending her an occasional love note can work wonders for your relationship as well. After all, we all love to be appreciated and acknowledged. So, make it an appointment to do this.

Making Memories

You don't have to consciously struggle to create memories. Instead, the most cherished memories are the ones that happen without any planning. When it comes to making memories, there are two things you must concentrate on. The first aspect is to bond with your baby. The second aspect is to think of family activities during your baby's first year. Even incredibly simple activities can not only make your baby happy, but they create memories you can cherish too. They help to strengthen the bond you share. Parental attachment, especially during the infant and toddler period, creates a positive relationship for life. The foundation you lay right now sets the tone for all future relationships.

For example, some simple activities you can use to bond with your baby and make memories are to help them choose their favorite toy and play fun games. Helping your baby choose their favorite toy is quite an exciting activity. It's quite likely they have received plenty of toys and other playthings from neighbors, friends, family members, and other well-wishers. Now, you simply need to layout all these toys in front of your baby and notice the toys they reach out for the most. Repeat this several times with all the toys and you will recognize a clear favorite.

Don't forget to document this process. From taking pictures to writing down the process of picking their favorite toys, then keep it with you. One fine day, you can tell your grown-up child about their favorite toy as a baby and show them pictures.

Another incredibly exciting activity is to collect handprints. The entire family can come together for this activity and press their print onto the porch, deck, or even papers. The papers or the cardstock can be framed later. This is not only a fun activity but it creates memories too. Every year, make it a family ritual or tradition of making handprints. Don't let go of an opportunity to record how tiny their hands are. You and your child can one day look back and be surprised at how small they once were.

Apart from handprints documentation, don't forget to take plenty of pictures. Whether it is selfies, pictures with filters, videos, or anything else along these lines — do it! Capture as much of this time as you can.

A simple yet exciting means to bond with your baby is to play games with them. A simple game is peekaboo or "Where is your nose?". These are two incredibly popular games and pretty much everyone knows about them — and for good reason. Whenever you are playing with your baby ensure you make the most of it. You will begin to recognize the different signs they are sending to indicate it's time to play. Whether it is smiling and reaching out for you or watching you or anyone else with interest shows they want to play. Apart from this, you should also know when it is time to take a break and your infant has had enough. If they start crying, spitting, or looking away, it means they have had enough.

Playing peekaboo is quite simple. This is an easy game that all infants are interested in. You need to hide your face behind your hands, move them away while saying the phrase, "peek-a-boo!" Babies take about 9 months to realize that even if your face is covered, you are still there. This is why they are fascinated by the simple disappearing and reappearing act this game provides. Once the baby starts understanding again, chances are they will try to reach out or touch you.

A simple yet effective and fun activity to help your baby develop their language skills while making them giggle is to play, "Where is your nose?" Ensure that you use a sing-song voice while saying "where is your nose?". After this, gently touch their nose and say, "There is your nose." Do this with genuine excitement. Keep repeating this game and use it to teach different parts of their body. Babies are inquisitive and can grasp concepts easily. Playing games allows you to teach your baby something new.

Spending time together as a family is extremely important. This is a great way to not just bond with your baby but your partner as well. After consulting your baby's pediatrician, you can determine when it is safe to start taking your baby outdoors. While indoors, different activities can still be done. For instance, art projects, small games, or creating indoor and outdoor sensory bins. A sensory bin is quite an exciting activity. Collect a bin that's big enough to hold multiple objects. Place different objects in it of varying textures such as feathers, balls, Lego bricks, slime, and so on. Ensure the objects are big enough so the baby cannot swallow them. This will help the baby learn how to pick up objects while learning about different textures.

Similarly, you can make art projects at home. Whether you are taking the handprints or footprints of your baby or using them to make something else, encourage them to start exploring different activities. After all, it is about having fun together.

Another simple yet effective means to bond with your baby is by singing. Singing is a stressbuster and certainly should not be limited to their bedtime. Instead, try singing in a happy tone to your baby. Chances are the baby will also try imitating you, and this will help build that language and speaking skills.

You can go for our family visit to the zoo and show all the different animals to your baby, visit a local library, go to the nearby park, spend a day at the beach, or even go for a stroll after every meal. The idea is to help your baby interact with the external world environment.

Some Moments to Capture

The first days, weeks, months, and even the first year will be gone before you realize it. Any parent, especially those with grown-up kids will tell you different milestones from listening to their first words to their first tooth. Still, the memories fade away unless recorded. As your baby grows, their curiosity to learn more about their arrival increases. Whenever you want to share, wouldn't it be better if you could remember all the details? If you are unsure of the different milestones to capture, go through the list given here.

Birth

The birth of your baby will be one of the most important moments in your life. The arrival of your baby will trigger a whirlwind of emotions and it can be extremely overwhelming and even tiring. The simplest way to ensure you never forget a single moment is to make a note of everything you experienced and everyone present. From the doctors and nurses who helped with the delivery to your friends and family members present.

First Day Home

Regardless of whether you believe it is a big or a small occasion to bring your baby home, ensure you capture every moment of it. Take plenty of videos and pictures so when the time comes to tell your child stories about their first day's home, you can show them! This helps create a more meaningful and visual storytelling experience.

First Encounters With Friends and Family

Friends, family members, and other loved ones might be extremely curious to meet your baby. Whenever they do, ensure you record their first meeting. These are extremely important and special moments, so recording it will give your little one a box full of memories shared with their loved ones.

Photos With Parents

It is not just about capturing moments your little one meets friends or family members. Ensure you get plenty of pictures with your baby too, especially during their first year. While doing this, you can add a few anecdotes or even stories next to the pictures. This creates more shared experiences as you go through parenthood.

Bath Time

An important moment most forget about or don't pay attention to is the first bath their baby has. This might feel insignificant, but over the years, this will become a cherished memory. Even if you cannot capture the first bath, ensure you do the subsequent ones.

First Smile or Laugh

The first smile or laugh is one moment most parents eagerly wait for, but it usually happens within the blink of an eye. It is certainly tricky to capture that slight smile or laugh that melts your heart. Capturing it on the reel is a truly special occasion. Even if you cannot, make sure that you keep the camera handy to capture the next smile. Even making a general note of when the baby smiled for the first time.

First Crawl

Your baby will learn to crawl sooner than you expect. Within no time, your bundle of joy will go from learning to move just their arms to crawling. As mentioned, some babies start crawling sooner than others. That said, your baby's pediatrician will give you the developmental milestones and the usual age they happen in. Use it as a guide and always keep the camera ready!

Waving

Something as simple as waving their arms is extremely exciting for babies. So, don't forget to capture your little bundle of joy waving their arms eagerly.

Learning to Stand and Walk

If you manage to record or capture the moment your baby learns to stand or take their first steps, pat yourself on the back.

New Friendships

Some friendships are forever. The friends your baby makes in their infancy might become their lifelong friends. So, capture moments when your baby meets other babies.

Playtime

The collection of toys your baby has will grow with them. They will also be interested in a few toys more than others. Find their favorites. And so the first time you play a game with your baby. Record it. For instance, it could be something as simple as peek-a-boo.

Important Holidays and Events

Don't forget to capture all the first holidays in your baby's life. Whether it is Easter or Christmas, capture them all.

Capturing and Preserving Precious Moments

Remembering to record and save all the moments becomes slightly difficult once the baby arrives. This is why you need physical and digital mementos so the memories you cherish can always be remembered. The simplest way to do this is by using a memory jar, taking a picture or video, maintaining the journal, writing a letter, and creating a shadow box full of mementos.

Taking a picture or video is the quickest way to ensure you have plenty of mementos of your loved ones. Whenever you are taking any videos or pictures, try using the burst feature on most smartphones to ensure you get the perfect shot.

Maintaining a journal might take a little bit of extra effort, but it is worth it. It is a great way to not just remember the memories created, but recollect them properly as well. Every year, make it a point to write a letter to your child on their birthday. Perhaps these letters can be bundled up and gifted to them on their 18th birthday or any other special occasion.

Creating and maintaining a memory jar is also a wonderful idea. Talk to any parent and chances are they wish they could have kept track of some funny things their child said or all the fun the family had over the years. This is where a memory jar comes into the picture. It is a decorated mason jar with a notepad and pen next to it. Whenever something worth remembering happens, simply make a note of it and put it in the jar.

A shadowbox essentially refers to a picture frame where things other than photos can be saved. You can add little details such as the positive pregnancy test result, hospital band, or even the first ultrasound of your baby.

Conclusion

Once you become a father, your life changes forever. This Is one responsibility that brings immense satisfaction. Also, this is the one role you will never truly stop playing regardless of your child's age. From now on, you are not only responsible for yourself, but another life too. From bringing your baby home to watching them grow, especially through their first year, you will experience a variety of changes. As you see your baby experience and do things for the first time, there are plenty of milestones you won't even want to forget. There will be plenty of picture-perfect memories that you will gather and cherish for the rest of your life. It's not just your life that has changed forever, even your partner is going to experience these changes.

In this book, you were given all the information needed to learn about everything that awaits you in your baby's first year. Apart from this, you were also given plenty of suggestions, practical advice, and tips that will support the progress through all these changes safely and healthily. Welcoming parenthood and becoming a parent are experiences unlike any other. The moment you hold your baby for the first time, you will realize how wonderful it truly is. After going through all the information given in this book, I trust you feel better prepared to deal with parenthood as a new father than before. Any worries, concerns, fears, or anxieties you had about becoming a father will also be reduced. From learning to handle your newborn baby such as bringing them home, feeding, and bathing them, to taking care of them; this book will act as your guide every step of the way.

You were also introduced to suggestions that will help become the hands-0n father your baby needs and the spouse your partner deserves.

Dear dad, stop worrying about making mistakes or doing something wrong while handling your baby. There are no hard and fast rules when it comes to parenting. It is a lifelong journey and a wonderful experience. As your baby grows, you will also need to grow as a parent. You don't have to worry about bonding with your baby because this will always happen as you become a hands-on father. Put your fears to rest and instead, keep a positive and open mind to everything that happens. This one year is going to be a roller coaster ride riddled with more happiness than you have ever experienced. Whenever you do something for the first time, chances are you get scared. This fear and anxiety are quite common and aren't out of the ordinary. Let go of any doubts that these fears reflect poorly on your parenting skills. Instead, it means you are human, and you certainly are not alone. Parenting is a process. There are no formulas to become excellent parents. Instead, it is a process of learning, trial and error, and improvement. As long as you are in it for the long haul, prepare yourself for an exhilarating journey.

Welcoming your baby home is going to be one of the most precious and unforgettable years of your life. You can become the best father for your baby and the best partner for your spouse with a little extra effort, patience, and love. All that you need to do is start following the advice given in this book!